W9-CFF-959

Doing Business in Japan

by Robert J. Ballon

Doing Business in Japan

Edited by ROBERT J. BALLON

PUBLISHED BY

SOPHIA UNIVERSITY, TOKYO

IN COOPERATION WITH

CHARLES E. TUTTLE COMPANY

RUTLAND VERMONT & TOKYO, JAPAN

REPRESENTATIVES
Continental Europe: BOXERBOOKS, INC., *Zurich*
British Isles: PRENTICE-HALL INTERNATIONAL, INC., *London*
Australasia: PAUL FLESCH & CO., PTY. LTD., *Melbourne*
Canada: m. g. hurtig ltd., *Edmonton*

Published by the Charles E. Tuttle Company, Inc.
of Rutland, Vermont & Tokyo, Japan
with editorial offices
at Suido 1-chōme, 2–6, Bunkyo-ku, Tokyo
in cooperation with
Sophia University
7, Kioi-chō, Chiyoda-ku, Tokyo

Copyright in Japan 1967, by Sophia University, all rights reserved

Library of Congress Catalog Card No. 67–21930
First Printing, 1967

Printed in Japan

PETER BROGREN, THE VOYAGERS' PRESS, TOKYO

Introduction

JAPANESE managers are very much aware of the need for management development, and hardly a week passes without several seminars being offered by specialized organizations. Top and middle management are particularly keen to familiarize themselves with the most advanced management techniques practiced or experimented with in other industrial countries. Their own business ways, however are, left unwritten and little analyzed since, after all, "This is Japan."

The foreign businessman residing in Japan feels much less privileged. Several years ago, or just a few weeks ago, he stepped gingerly on to Japanese soil, equipped with a solid dose of goodwill and an even bigger dose, he felt, of business acumen. Often his goodwill has worn thin, and his acumen has developed a bitter edge. He finds himself between the devil and the deep blue sea. The home office has little sympathy for the "This is Japan" leitmotive which dots his reports, except for sending out a V.I.P. who easily "solves" problems in a perfunctory way. Saddled with these new "solutions," the local representative dejectedly plunges back into the "Sea of the Unknown" of Japanese business behavior. Holding his head bravely (and hopefully) above water, he struggles along...

This volume is dedicated to those businessmen who, anxious to increase their knowledge of Japanese business methods, have manifested the desire to better equip themselves for international business in Japan.

Early in 1965, the Sophia University Socio-Economic Institute started International Management Development Seminars with a so-called Business in Japan Workshop. This Workshop has been repeated ten times, and has been attended by over 300 foreign businessmen representing 17 nationalities. Some of the working papers used during the workshop have been compiled into this volume.

In Part I, the background is presented from two different angles: firstly the psychological picture, an explanation of Japanese thought processes, and secondly the historical-economic picture of the infancy and growth of the modern Japanese economy.

Part II studies the present Japanese economy. Articles analyze the apparent failure of the fiscal policy in the 1960's, the fate of small and medium sized enterprises, the problems of the capital market, and consumer satisfaction.

Following this panorama of the economy, Part III tackles the subtleties of the Japanese business scene. Here, especially, we note vivid differences from the West.

Finally, the appendix lists and comments on significant tables and graphs.

Acknowledgments

THE editor wishes to express his gratitude to the staff of the seminars, university professors and business executives, all of them enthusiastic supporters of better business relations for better international understanding. Special credit must be given to Robert K. Paus, Assistant Professor of Business Administration, who edited the earlier drafts of some of the working papers, to Jean-Pierre Lehmann, a student in Far Eastern Affairs, and Simon Virgo, who reviewed the manuscript and improved it substantially. Our gratitude goes also to our secretaries who have unfailingly taken care of the administrative details of the seminars, and the repeated typing of the working papers.

List of Authors

ABAD, Jose M.: *Professor of Economics, Sophia University.*

AKAMATSU, Teisuke: *Attorney at Law, Professor of Japanese Law, Sophia University.*

BAIRY, Maurice: *Professor of Psychology, Sophia University.*

BALLON, Robert J.: *Professor of Economics, Sophia University, Co-Director of the Sophia University Socio-Economic Institute, Seminar Director of the International Management Development Seminars.*

HATTORI, Ichirō: *Director, Daini Seikō Watch Co.*

JOHNSTON, George D. Jr.,: *Former Manager, J. Walter Thompson Japan, Ltd.*

PAUS, Robert K.: *Lecturer of Business Administration, Sophia University.*

SAITO, Kinichirō: *Professor of Statistics and Marketing, Sophia University.*

TAKAMIYA, Susumu: *Professor of Business Administration, Sophia University.*

TERAOKA, T.W.M.: *Partner, Peat, Marwick, Mitchell & Co.*

TERASAWA, Yoshio: *Manager, Foreign Department, Nomura Securities Co.*

Contents

PART THREE: BUSINESS

Part One

BACKGROUND

INTRODUCTION

IN ANY *society there are certain patterns, formulae and customs which guide not only the external aspect of life, but also the thought process. To understand the business* modus vivendi, *one must understand action and its reaction.*

As markets develop and business horizons expand in the complex world of the late twentieth century, more attention has to be paid not only to the organizational structures as they stand, but also to their operation. To understand any organization, it is essential to have some understanding of the individuals within it. The function of a foreign company's representative in any country is, in fact, to be that company's ambassador, taking into consideration native sensitivities, reactions, and so on.

The rest of this volume deals with the external aspects of the Japanese economic world; this article explores the intricacies of Japanese society, and how it has become what it is. Starting with the embryonic stage—the family-child relationship—this article deals successively with the development of the organism, and finally explains the personalities viewed within the general framework.

CHAPTER I
Japanese Ways

by Maurice Bairy

JAPANESE WAYS

The Family-Child Relationship—The Psychology of the Japanese—Structure of the Organism—The Growth of the Organism—The Rhythm of Development—Interrelationship Within the Organism—Application to Group Dynamics—The Terms of Interrelationship (Authority and Responsibility, Decision-making, Command)

As a general introduction to Japanese behavior, it is interesting to compare how a baby is introduced into the world in Japan and in the West. At birth, the Western baby is separated from his mother; his subsequent development is concerned with the re-conquest of his mother, through submission and a certain self-denial. Alone in his crib, he is surrounded by people who look down at him and from whom he gets little sympathy unless he refrains from tantrums and crying. Everything is done, in other words, so that the child may learn how to be himself by recognizing others. The baby learns that there is a world of persons he must reckon with in order to satisfy his desires, and that there is a world of things he must explore in order to realize his own limits. Everything concerns the development of a rather independent and self-sufficient individual, who is, nevertheless, required to maintain close contact with the world of persons and things.

In Japan, on the contrary, birth changes only the nature of the child's unity with his mother. Instead of being inside the womb, he is outside, but still so close that there is hardly any break in the mother-child unity. The baby is constantly near his mother, and when she is lying down on the *tatami* he is also near everyone else in the family. A new child in Japan is the most important member of the family.

Whereas the Western child is left to himself, the Japanese baby lives with his mother, without any separate "point of view." The Japanese room usually lacks furniture or other ornaments which would excite the curiosity of the child, as do the ornaments, the windows, the mirrors, the thousand objects which scintillate in a Western room. The child's view is limited to the close family group, in which everyone emulates everyone else, which gives him a feeling of well-being. He develops an attitude which he will have all through his life—the need to be dependent, the wish to be loved. We can see the same need in the Western child, but it is manifested in another way. Whereas the Western child, in his isolation, is forced to deny his independence in order to survive, the Japanese child experiences through the solicitude of all the members of the group the interdependence of all. He is not conscious of it yet, of course; he will become aware of it when he is about one year old, but his existence itself is constantly conditioned by this necessity, which gives him the greatest satisfaction. He will be happy insofar as he allows himself to become the object of a subordinating love. His whole being is the being of the whole. Winning love or demanding love seems to be one difference between the Western and the Japanese child.

Our aim is not to present a psychology of the Japanese child, but only to stress the difference in orientation. Whereas the Western child has a certain initiative, the Japanese child is dependent upon everything and everyone. The system of relationships which is considered by Westerners as a kind of glorious conquest, as a progressive emergence of the "I," is envisaged by the Japanese as gradual immersion in society. Both are look-ing for the self and this self is identical, namely a more or less perfect participation in existence, but the one seeks it through a conscious personalization, the other through an unconscious socialization. The ideal of both is to play a role: in the West, attention is focused upon the player of the role; in Japan, it is the society which receives credit for the performance of the individual.

Another consideration in this primary mother-child relationship is the great difficulty Japanese have in considering a person or a fact in an objective way, the common attitude of a Western subject toward an object. Many foreigners complain about the Japanese lack of understanding of "obvious facts." It is quite common for Japanese to confront the presentation of, let us say, economic problems with an attitude of refusal. Westerners show, for instance, that to take this or that step of trade liberalization would be advantageous to the Japanese themselves. Although the argumentation seems as clear as spring water, the Japanese remain adamant.

More concretely, a logical demonstration made to the Japanese which has been punctuated by a "yes" of assent all along is suddenly concluded by the Japanese with the disappointing *wakaranai*. He really means. "It is quite all right, but it is irrelevant; your conclusion is not fitting!" Our great error has been to pull the problem out of its concrete context; the Japanese, had he an articulate Western mind, could say "You are quite right if you solve this problem rationally, but that does not have anything to do with the concrete situation which is much more complex and much more involved." The Westerner tries to be as objective as possible, because he can take a point of view; the Japanese, on the contrary, is involved in a maze of relationships which cannot be broken, which must be maintained at any cost. As soon as we ask the Japanese what he thinks about a particular subject we reach a deadlock, because he does not think. What we mean is that the Japanese individual cannot "isolate" himself in order to consider the question only rationally. He is too much involved with others and with Japan, to be able to express an opinion about it. The whole of Japan has to adapt itself to each new situation, and the solution will be the reaction of the whole to the threat of disequilibrium. If we Westerners are sincere, we agree that the solutions to the cases proposed by the Harvard Business School look intelligent and exhaustive, but we also know very well that the circumstances will impose many corrections to their theoretical settlement. The Japanese approach is more total, but also much more confusing and maybe less universal.

Another consequence is opportunism and infrequent adjustment to all the obstacles brought up by the march of events. The mother-child relationship is constant and not subordinated to another's will. The child gets whatever he wants, whenever he desires it. In the same way, the adult solves problems as they present themselves. That is one of the reasons why experience is so esteemed in Japan. The one who can solve the problems is the one who has already solved many of them.

A word like *maturity* is confusing. Maturity, for foreigners, means restraining oneself from decisions or actions which do not conform to a long-range goal. The Japanese, through his immediate answers to concrete situations, acquires wisdom. It is rather difficult to distinguish between maturity and wisdom, but let us note that in the West experience is often lacking even in people who are called mature.

The study of the mother-child relationship could reveal many more characteristics of Japanese behavior. This illustration, however, was given only to establish the wholesome character of Japanese psychology. We cannot separate the child from his mother, or the family from its whole environment; in the same way, we are forced to consider Japan and her inhabitants as a gigantic organism where men and things form a unity it would be dangerous and erroneous to break, if we want to understand it.

Psychology of the Japanese

Technology has influenced the Japanese psychology only for about a hundred years. One can therefore surmise that the Japanese have developed some psychological trends which were precisely the ones neglected by other peoples under the impact of scientific development. There has been a tendency to oppose both mentalities, instead of an effort to look at both as two ways of expressing the same universal human mentality. Our attitude should be that the Western way of looking at persons and things is not the only way, and that our prejudices against the Japanese way, for instance, may be due to the fact that our culture is directed by the idea of efficiency. There are two very different ways of looking at things. These attitudes have been characterized as "reality-directed" or "utility-directed"; we can look at things for what they are or for the convenience they offer us. Our civilization makes us rather interested in the utility of things. To use a trivial example, we eat almost without tasting anything, and what the dietitian tell us to eat; the Japanese, on the other hand, show much more interest in the way the food is presented than in the food itself.

The knowledge of the Japanese is thus modeled upon the relationships which exist between living beings; it is a constant alertness to the ambient milieu through a steady communication and exchange. To know is to be related, to live with, to share the same destiny. The proximity and the immediacy of contact suppress this opposition of subject-object, which is the basis of Western thought, and also reduce the distribution of acquaintanceships during a certain period of time. Knowledge is unity from the beginning; it might be said that knowledge is simply awareness of a relationship which until now was only lived. This awareness is as sudden as lightning. Therefore one cannot expect from the Japanese some self-criticism or some motivation which, in the Western sense, supposes an abstraction and the introduction of a mathematical time based upon the division of space. Living in such close proximity to everything around, the Japanese cannot expect anything but the "happening" of a world he does not perceive rationally, but with which he lives intensely. The ideal is to live, and to live is an experience which is always new and always different. You never breathe the same air twice. From the beginning, the Japanese have developed this sympathy for reality, the reality as it is, not as it is conceived or tagged by the human mind. Could we call this situation "sympathy"? The word may be misleading. Actually, there is a "growing together," excluding any attitude which could be interpreted on the part of man as condescending to share an experience with beings of an inferior order. Persons and things are both called in Japanese "objects" *(mono)*. There is a luxuriant system of relationships so complete and essential that it is impossible to evade it or to liberate oneself from it.

Since the Meiji period, Japanese have gone abroad to study; in recent years, this movement has been intensified. It has always puzzled Westerners who have had these apprentices in their offices or schools to see that these bearers of the Western enlightenment were, most of the time, relegated to a subaltern function once they returned to their own places of work. People who had shown talents as responsible executives during their period of training were now low employees, without apparently having any opportunity of putting their foreign experience to use. There is, it seems, no other justification for this behavior than the necessity for re-rooting the organism and starting again the process of syn-activity with and within the whole. It is easily understandable that it is very difficult for a foreign element not only to be accepted in this complex, but even to be accounted for. Only through long familiarization and assimilation will the foreigner be considered.

One of the surprises met by the foreign businessman who wants to conduct "business" in Japan is to be submitted to a series of questions which establish his various relationships with wife, children, and the management of the firm concerned. Is the man we Japanese are dealing with "related" to the world of things and persons? In other words, are we dealing with another living organism whose truth and strength is verified by the multiplicity of ties which a strong living being necessarily contracts? This time-consuming process of questioning is not precisely verification of information, but rather getting to know the man as he *is*. Who can say that he knows somebody just by looking at his name card? Besides, the whole group must get to know the new element, and to the great bewilderment of the foreigner, his interlocutors change practically with every meeting. The Japanese are not impenetrable—they can be inter-pollinated.

The whole structure of Japan can thus be considered as a gigantic living organism in which each part is playing a role, but where there is no place for an outsider. The possibility of establishing a methodology for this research presents itself here. It appears from the above that one cannot singularize one individual or one thing in Japan, because nothing has value by itself, but only in its relation to other things. It is also impossible to analyze a concept in the perspective of Japanese culture because of the risk of losing at least half of the content.

"Religion," for instance, applied to the Japanese is either unverifiable or deprived of any sense. Nevertheless, the Japanese *are* religious. In the same way when they talk about leadership, competition, motivation, and so on, they use the word, but the meaning is different. Enthralled with the beauty of their island, the fertility of their soil, the marvel of their climate, they have developed a concrete knowledge of the world which brings them nearer to nature than anybody else.

This unity is realized through harmonious interrelationship, but the process of unification finds its source in the origin of life. To accommodate the flow of life, the structure articulates itself vertically from the source into the various affluents.

The Structure of the Organism

The Japanese make their way in the world through acquaintance and familiarity. This net of relationships constitutes a structure which allows them to find their way through the maze of reality, distinguishing the useful, the beautiful, the medicinal, the clean, and all the various elements which make life enjoyable and provide security. Quite spontaneously, they center their aspirations upon this life which reveals itself so multifariously around them. They model themselves upon the image they see day after day. The young tree grows in the shadow of the older tree, the vegetation feeds on the neighboring water, the sea progressively reveals its wealth to the more adventurous—all are examples of subordination of the small to the great, the young to the old. Adjusting thmselves to the rhythm of nature, they find out about death and life and the instability of everything. The present moment will never come again and promises only evanescent delight. The splendor of the cherry blossom is also the triumph of decay; the moment of its glory marks its death. At a higher level, the meeting of a friend is the announcement of his departure. The greatest risk is to live.

But life is exacting. There are rules which cannot be forgotten without resulting in death or disequilibrium. Nature commands not only a ritual, but also a whole system of relationships through which the energy of life flows more or less abundantly in proportion to the acceptance of the various bonds which bind as well as promote development. In a culture where the concrete and its perception are prevalent, a hierarchical structure is as natural as it is necessary. You do not transplant with impunity a plant from a rich soil to sand, and you cannot expect a tree to grow without water. Everything is set and observances are numerous. Acquaintance with the world is, on the one hand, awe-inspiring: volcanoes, typhoons, earthquakes are everyday experiences and are terrifying; but, on the other hand, they are natural, so that some kind of connivance has been established between nature and themselves. Japan, in fact, bathes in a climate which could be called sacred. The "unknown" is tolerated and accepted along the whole scale of situations, so the word that may be the most used in Japanese is *wakaranai,* a term which could be translated as "there is no explanation." Things are taken as they are, and there is very little criticism, although experience or use is a permanent criterion of value. To expect a rebellion, which in other countries would be called an initiative, is contrary to the general attitude of acceptance. In this constant contact with things, due to the vigilant and loving attention given to whatever exists, a fortuitous complex of things can reveal itself interesting and constitute an "invention." The Japanese do not imitate things; they accept things as they are, look at them, play with them with their eyes, their hands, their ears, all their senses, and make out of them something quite similar to the model, but there is always something new added. Maybe there is only one screw where there were two; maybe tin is used instead of steel; this change, though, results not from voluntary design, but from a new disposal. They have made an .object simpler and cheaper, not with the intention of so doing, but because through trial and error they have reproduced through and by their own means an object which was the fruit of an idea materialized.

Contrary to mythological tradition, there was no "Creation" for the Japanese: the world was there and, for a mentality which has not been touched by metaphysics or which is perhaps more open to the concrete aspects of the world, the best and most sensible attitude is one of submission and demission. This process is not foreign to the definition of invention by H. Poincaré, who insists on groping, repetition, multiple distribution and redistribution of elements in an apparent darkness and ignorance of the final result. The strict logic of the West and, accordingly, the systematic study of previous data, accelerates the final step, but it is the same confrontation with the concrete which is the basis of discovery.

This loving propinquity with things, this familiarity with his surroundings, could be called esthetic perception, for somebody who did not develop the Westerner's agility and ease of abstract thought. The Japanese perceive the surrounding world through the senses, and with such an intimacy that it is a perpetual enchantment. The world for the Japanese is not a confusion, a hubbub to be organized, but a thing of beauty to be admired. This affirmation calls for an immediate correction to the accusation of materialism made against this group of esthetes. Indeed, in the world of business, it seems that the appetite for gain and competition is law. The truth is that in the domain of objects reduced to their role of tools, this trend of Western mentality prevails, but this trait far from describes the total attitude of the Japanese. The meeting of subject with object could be described, for the Japanese, as an exposure; for foreigners, as reorganization of their perception and their motivation. In other words, the dialogue in the Western sense between two interlocutors is not possible, but first a method of exchange which is common to both must be found. The Westerner is not confronted with a system of ideas, but with another world, or rather a world which does not develop according to his pattern. This attitude should not be interpreted as community pride or exacerbated nationalism, but as the expression of an organism reacting to an exterior element. Only the "fact of getting accustomed" will favor more intimate communication.

Just as the Westerner is tempted to reject the Japanese or to condemn their ways without being patient enough to harmonize himself with them, so some impatient Japanese, chiefly in the literary world, would like to reject all foreign influence and develop a strong national feeling. As a natural fruit of this exposure to the West, in fact, some Japanese have developed an awareness of themselves similar to the national feelings of Western peoples. This sense for their country is completely different from the pre-war and war nationalism, which was a kind of racial movement. It is the individual reaction of a few who have had contact with the West, who are impregnated with its ideas and who pave the way for the first interchange at the conceptual level between the two worlds. Although Japan is centered on herself, the day this intimate contact with her inner self requires that Japan, in order to be Japan, must be international, on that day Japan will be international in the full sense of the word.

To the Japanese, knowledge is not the Western absorption of the outside into the inner self through some kind of reduction of the sensible qualities; it is a penetration, a coaction, a coexistence with the world of persons and things. Metaphysical properties do not interest the Japanese, who are enthralled with the quality of whatever surrounds them. The Japanese are always in a state of rapture with things. The Westerners question the world, and keep wondering "why?" This "why" is one of the few attitudes which get on the nerves of the Japanese. The Westerners build, conquer, organize; the Japanese shelter themselves, obey, take a delight in whatever they see in the new corner of the maze they incessantly go through. In this perspective, the best guarantee of the existence of things is their affective perception. For the Japanese to know is "to be with." By co-being, by co-growing, by co-developing with nature, they realize this unity, which is the aim of any epistemological theory.

To remain stable, this interrelationship needs harmony, a constant solidarity of all with all, and that is what must be maintained at all costs. Without this vertical movement in life, the Japanese cannot live; to have the communication cut is to cease to exist (a slight difference from death, which is just another aspect of nature). The tendency of the Japanese is always to maintain contact in spite of everything, and to avoid reaching an extreme crisis.

Efforts to introduce democracy to Japan have mostly taken the form of discussions, forums and the like, with the secret or open intention of the promoters to create a clear, definite conviction of the benefits of democracy and the evil of any other system. The results have been disappointing. The Japanese were delighted to meet and to discuss. They enjoy being together and talking over every possible topic. But they do not meet *in order* to arrive at a result, or to reach a decision. The foreigners present at such meetings leave with the impression that nothing has been achieved. And they are right! But nothing more could have been achieved, since everything is set forever.

Their "discussion" is not our discussion. While they are exchanging appreciations of the various aspects of the question, all of which are acceptable, all true, the foreigners are confronting one another with contradictory statements. The opposition of no and yes is purely logical. In nature, we could repeat the old saying: "nothing is lost, nothing is gained." There is no plain yes or no. This lack of a clear answer is a constant frustration to the foreigner, but can we say that the intellectual satisfaction of a short statement gives us lasting satisfaction? Answers which theoretically are most satisfactory are in reality of very little avail. For the Japanese a discussion is an opportunity to experiment, to circulate opinions, to communicate the various views of the members toward the subject considered. Nothing else can be expected other than shared information about the topic discussed; it is, so to speak, a technique for reinforcing the solidarity of the group.

We have a tendency "to make the situation clear," as we say, and that is usually achieved by exclusion. If the partner does not agree, it is too bad; we cannot get along and we part. Often, though, we feel we must reestablish relations, even at the cost of great effort and humiliation. The Japanese never think of breaking or even of weakening. The result is the same, although the method is different.

The need for contact and the anxiety of not breaking it are the rules of social conduct, with a predominantly vertical dimension; each member of the group always expresses his dependence upon another member.

Another aspect of communication is the importance of circumstances, the ritualistic aspect of the communication. The language itself could shed some light on this, but the Japanese are not very interested. As good estheticians they expect the rules to be observed and the forms to be respected. If you are a teacher or a man with some authority, you are not supposed to tell jokes unless they are pointedly and explicitly introduced.

In the same vein, the Japanese do not go to *Noh* to see or hear something new, but to enjoy the way it is said. The whole thing looks like an obstacle race one must complete without falling. Foreigners remain dumbfounded at the prolonged exchange of polite formulae which always take five minutes of every meeting, but the Japanese appreciate the skill with which one goes through this kind of exercise on the flying trapeze!

Another testimony to the meaning of close contact is the importance given to the departure or the return of a member of the group. The platforms of all the railway stations of Japan are crammed with groups bowing very formally to departing travelers; for a big director, the whole staff is present; for one child leaving to study in the great city, all the members of the family attest physically and emotionally to their participation in the separation.

We tend to criticize or deplore the intricacy and complexity of human relations, for instance, in business firms. In our society, however, where efficiency is submitted to competition and ambition, the great problem of social equilibrium remains. Efficiency is not an end in itself; it should be viewed in terms of destiny, of which human unity is a part. Japanese values could contribute to this ideal.

The Growth of the Organism

In investigating the psychological process, we must distinguish between fundamental motivation and its elicited expression. For Westerners, the reasons for an action constitute the motivation. The motivation only finds expression in the so-called reasons, which intellectually satisfy the enquiring mind, and enhance the personality. Since, in Japan, this aspect is secondary, it is hardly surprising that although we do not find explicit reasons, we must recognize a global and general motivation.

Because of this constant symbiosis with the whole, the Japanese do not have *goals* in our sense. Goal, in our language, means the projection of a program, an objective set up logically and rationally. The motivation of the Japanese must be looked for at a less specific level, where it is not formulated abstractly. It is, thus, an unconscious motivation which we can only surmise in concrete experience—an intention which reveals itself in the activity of Japan. Whatever is good for the group should be done;

whatever could make the whole greater and healthier should be achieved. The motivation is a condition of dissociation and tension which constitutes every moment of Japanese life. Each reduction of tension or recovery of integrity is submitted to a new disequilibrium and leads progressively to the greater development of the whole.

Some foreigners think that on account of the necessity and the pressure of financial and economic exchange, the Japanese must finally rationalize their motivation, and run their business on a profit basis. That would require a great transformation of the Japanese mentality, probably not exactly in the sense the Westerners expect, because the motivation of the Japanese is more complex and rich. The unconscious is the source of our motives, and Western theoreticians, arguing on the purpose of the enterprise, are still divided between the motives of gain, of progress, of civilization, or the possibility of creativity. It seems that no synthesis of these various aspects has been achieved. The Japanese, without knowing, verify all these goals in their spontaneous and natural development. As has been indicated already, for the Japanese the function of an enterprise is the survival and the growth of Japan.

What is this whole? It is Japan. Not the Japan of Yamato or Ise, not the Japan of Meiji, but the Japan of today, which, in order to exist, must be related to the whole world. Japan is indeed the motivation and intention of the collectivity. This Japan is a Japan interested in playing a role in the world. It is no longer the role of an isolationist or nationalist Japan, but an Asian representative in the world community.

There is a tendency among Japanese to deny the influence of the past upon the here-and-now. For many of them, past is past. Psychologically, this can be explained by the exigency of the present which requires all their attention. The old roots are interesting, but only inasmuch as the tree is asserting its new vigor to react against wind and sun. The attention to the present attests indirectly to the faithfulness to the past. The attention to the present supposes a permanent obligation of readjusting, reshaping or re-tuning the new situation with the whole. Just as the purpose of a tree is to develop all the eventualities of its essence, the purpose of Japan is to realize all its potentialities. The success of adaptation can be equated to the fulfillment of this goal. That may be the explanation of the quality which is praised by foreigners, but often misinterpreted. The Japanese adapt themselves not through cunningness or plotting or political machination, but through a spontaneous answer to the exigencies of life. The Westerner's life can be seen as a series of problems, and the life of the Japanese as a continuous solicitude. The Westerner must cope with logical riddles solved with the help of reason or mathematics. There are no insoluble problems since we have all the data for their solution.

We are very proud of our achievements in this area, although we notice quite often that our theoretical answers do not have much value in practice. We are very grateful to computers which allow us to take account of many variables which better define reality. The Japanese are, again and again, confronted by new situations. It is quite normal that the growth and the development of an organism are not realized without pain and anxiety. With every new situation, the system of relationships is disrupted and must be reset harmoniously in order that the flow of communication or the interrelationship may function freely again.

In business, the management of an enterprise or an organization requires a constant reappraisal of the actual situation. If the director retires, the whole hierarchy must be reconsidered to re-establish harmony. If a tree, in its growth, encounters an obstacle, a reorganization of its whole self is necessary to allow it to bend or follow another pattern; all the cells are affected by this change. The way of reappraisal is called *chokkan* by the Japanese, a concrete intuition of everyday experience. This accounts for the rhythm of the Japanese economy. The actual conditions of the market force a reconsideration of the productivity schedule.

The immediate implication is that very little planning, or only short-term planning, is possible in this context. The present situation seems to be the determining factor. Along with adaptation to successive disturbances, through trial and error, the body continues to live according to its ambiguous and natural destiny. In other words, the Japanese are not solving problems, because such an attitude would assume the possibility of an abstraction which is impervious to them. Everything and everybody is determined, but the schedule of the happening is unknown. Nature and unpredictability are the laws. The part of man is submission, not domination as implied in the Western attitude. Western psychology is somehow an apotheosis of the "I" and history is the slow but progressive domination of the world. In Japan, nature and man coexist and are a solidarity: nature is respected, not mastered. The Japanese are coping with facts and situations, not with ideas and systematizations. Confucianism, which has such a great influence upon Japanese society, does not have a theory about society, but simply tells how each individual should know and keep his place in society. The challenge is not to organize society or to perfect it: everything is fixed already; but it is very important to fulfill every task prescribed by life.

A theory of Japanese industrial relations, a system of Japanese organization, can only be expected at the cost of self-delusion. But it is possible to describe the natural and spontaneous activity of life or nature in an industrial setting.

The Rhythm of Development

The foreigner, for whom time is money, is at a loss when he sees how unimportant time is to the Japanese. It seems that the Japanese are never in a hurry and that nothing is more important than the present moment. The future does not seem to worry them much.

If the foreigner staying in Japan for a while reads articles on economics in the newspapers and magazines, he will notice that the situation is very often presented in terms of pending bankruptcy. How can we reconcile seeming indifference with this tight-rope walking, this imminence of catastrophe which looms over the economy?

If Japan can be likened to an organism, as I have tried to show, it is quite evident that she cannot be forced—in normal circumstances, at least—to grow or to assimilate a new element faster than is allowed by the laws of nature. One can only measure time here biologically—and the biological clock knows no urgency.

Since everything and everybody are subordinated to this rhythm, there is no point in getting excited about the speed of the process. It will take the time it needs and that is all. Similarly, it seems unwise to project or anticipate. We do not know how the organism will react to the various elements, and we know still less how it will grow and develop. As a living organism, the industrial organization is always subject to the eventuality of "indigestion" or too much "strain." The best performance will be to maintain equilibrium. If the organism shows signs of disequilibrium, of unnatural outgrowth, then there are reasons to be worried and to fear the worst. There is always a chance to go on living, but, if pressures or requirements are too many, there is a risk of death and extinction.

Another explanation of this indifference toward the future can be found in the book *Nihonjin no Shakai Shinri* by Tadashi Fukutake. The author points out precisely this sense of participation in the laws of nature, this resignation to the established order. Paradoxically, the Japanese confess their inability to change the future as well as to change the present. "This is the situation we have to face; it is inescapable. And the next situation will be exactly the same. Why worry about inevitable worries? Why be unduly concerned about the inevitable?"

Still another explanation of this indifference toward the future is given by Professor Inatomi. According to him, the Japanese do not have any notion of time because they do not have any notion of self. Indeed, time exists only by reference to a term, or definite extent. But, according to the Japanese conception, there is no term, there is only a continuous flow. There is no past, no future: time is what measures an action, or rather time is marked by the change of action. It seems that time is an immense reservoir from which you can help yourself. Time belongs to nobody, it is at the disposal of everybody. Everybody can dip and the supply is inexhaustible. Time is what marks life, chiefly the psychological life, which is run, as it has been surmised, by all the others. To appropriate time would be to make it "mine." To direct time supposes a self. Time is simply the dimension in which the Japanese live; they do not own it. This is one explanation for not keeping appointments, set with so much eagerness and seriousness. Time possesses them, not the contrary! It would be easy to comment lightly about the Japanese on their way to becoming the biggest watchmakers in the world (nevertheless aspiring to possess a Swiss watch, the symbol of exactitude) and to list stories about their traditional laxity in respecting the time of work, class or leisure. It seems that time marks a change of situation. According to the Western conception, time is a mathematical abstraction of the rational mind made to measure time. But, if we put ourselves in the Japanese mentality, according to which nothing arrives, but everything is determined from the beginning, nobody can change anything. Time registers only the change from one situation to another.

An example may help illustrate this point: A Japanese, waiting for a street-car, sees it down the street. The Japanese says "The tram has come"; the Westerner "The tram is coming." For the Japanese, the tram,

B

which belongs to the general situation, has appeared in the specific context, with an immediate connection to the person concerned. It fulfills an expectation concerning a fact which could not *not* happen. It was promised by the past, it was in the series of events to happen. In the Western perspective, things are different. Westerners state only the fact that something which was not there is going to be here.

The Japanese sanction or show their satisfaction and their agreement with what is happening, and what should have happened anyhow; the Westerners, faithful to their rational approach, deduce logically that if the streetcar is already seen, there is a great probability it will move progressively toward the next stop. Time, for the Japanese, is what punctuates the transition from unconsciousness to awareness. It seems that the past always expresses an accomplishment, like a man invited to a luxurious cruise who registers with joy the various experiences one by one. *Arigato gozaimashita, Gokuro sama deshita, Gochiso sama deshita,* all are expressions of satisfaction with some event which has fulfilled the expectancy: "It *has* been a great trouble," "It *has* been most difficult," etc.

One last consideration should be mentioned. Given the uncertainty of life and the risk which is the law of life, time is not a value; it punctuates only the relativity of everything. The only reality is the remembrance of a moment of joy, a moment of sadness, a moment of loneliness. All events are apprehended totally, not only intellectually, and therefore fall into the domain of psychological appreciation. In other words, the events take their importance from the way they affect the Japanese totally. The Japanese do not reckon with minutes, but with events in which they were involved.

Foreigners have wondered at the alternate moods of docility and violence of the Japanese. If they are partially explained by the consideration of intense group affiliation, they also find some justification in the commitment exacted by the circumstances of the moment considered. The element of mathematical time or of duration intervenes most of the time in Western reaction, except within the child or the criminal, and makes the Westerner "think" about the eventual consequences. An affront, a blame for the Japanese endangers his total life which is involved here and now; right now he must give an immediate solution, he draws his sword and he strikes. Once that provocation is solved, he is ready again to show real kindness.

In dealing with Japanese, the extremes have to be avoided. An open conflict can break the relationship, and it will take long and patient effort to come to a new understanding.

Interrelationship Within the Organism

Remote conditions must be respected. Thus no Japanese enters into contact with another Japanese unless properly introduced, just as no question is asked without having established its relationship with the context.

The importance of etiquette is constantly stressed; nobody simply tells the maid: "Dust this table!"; it must be explained that because there are special guests, or because you have seen that it was dusty, the table should be cleaned. This explains, to some extent, why every action in Japan seems to require much more time than in the West.

Immediate conditions of relationship must be respected, too. Since the group is more important than the individual, it is through the group that the introduction will be made. The way a Japanese introduces himself is not "My name is so-and-so"; first comes the name of the outfit or the group to which the individual belongs. He is *Mitsui Ginko no Tanaka*; he is "Tanaka working for the Mitsui Bank." The credentials are not his own but the ones of the group he is especially associated with.

As a matter of fact, an "I-Thou" relationship in the Western sense is almost unverifiable in Japan. This statement calls for an explanation, for there is perhaps no other society in the world where the word "friend" *(tomodachi)* is used more often. On the other hand, foreigners who have been in Japan for years, if they are acquainted with many Japanese, nevertheless complain about the lack of real friendship. Travelers or people associated with Japanese for years through business express their disappointment at the lack of intimacy in a country where hospitality is practiced so exquisitely, and where the exchange of presents seems to indicate a mutual devotion.

The probable answer is paradoxical. In general, the Japanese themselves do not know such friendships, and cannot allow themselves such involvement, because it would ruin the harmony of the group. Where the law of solidarity is a question of survival, a limited association of two or three would endanger smooth and free communication between all members of the community. Friends in Japan are not *my* friends; we belong to the same graduation class, the same university, the same firm. The individuality is all received from the group. The bond between a group of friends or associates is not something personal, but a reference to the group. We are friends not primarily because I know you, and you know me, or because we are both interested in electronics or in tennis; we are friends because we both work for the same company or play tennis at the same club. Personal relationships are possible only at a superficial level and if they become more intimate (for instance, the relationship with a geisha), they are condemned by the social rules, or rather they are sanctioned as extraordinary behavior.

This is so much true that the Japanese cannot think of a business relationship as a friendly relationship. The relationship is certainly as human as possible, including drinking and eating parties, but it does not have any connection with family relationships. How astonished foreigners are who, having welcomed Japanese in their homes abroad, have this treatment reciprocated when they come to Japan. They are not invited a second time, though. The Japanese have fulfilled a duty, but they are not ready to make it a custom.

In the business world, the meeting of a foreigner with Japanese is usually rather a trying experience. The foreigner is met by a group of people who all seem to have the same importance. The name cards are perfunctorily exchanged, and then starts the long procedure of establishing actual contact between the two interlocutors (the group and the individual). This progressive familiarization seems futile to the foreigner who wants to "get to the point." He will only do this, however, when many different members of the business firm he is dealing with have become acquainted with him. Quite spontaneously, when this fundamental concrete basis is realized, the agreement will be concluded. It must be said that this process can take years, and often discourages the foreigner. He cannot expect to discuss the project person to person; such an attitude would be relevant to an exchange at a logical level. The interpretation of decision-making in Japan corroborates this statement.

The whole process seems, to the foreigner, to indicate reluctance to deal with him, or to be some trial of his sincerity and seriousness. In reality, it reveals once more the Japanese way of communication. A living organism is selecting experimentally and progressively what could contribute to its development; that task can take months. As has been said already, there is no plan or system in the Japanese perspective; there is only a structure ready to react by adoption or rejection according to its natural necessities. One cannot expect them to act differently toward foreigners than they do toward themselves.

It is interesting to note how rigidity in following the rules can be relaxed, and a new pattern developed, little by little, in conformity with the basic nature of Japan. Japan—always open to whatever can help her growth—finds herself exposed to the necessity of accelerating her loan operations. Perception of this new fact is underlined by seeing foreign banks using this new procedure, and by having lost profits, or not having grown as much as had been expected. Reacting to this splinter in the skin, the Japanese will eventually change their methods, since the health of the whole exacts this new conditioning. The Japanese will adapt themselves to the exigencies of the West but it will be through practical intuition, not on account of some logical reflection.

This progressive assimilation is not only true in the above example, but is verifiable in many other aspects of modernization. The Japanese will adopt eventually what is suggested from outside, but they will do so in their own way and according to their own rhythm; materially the result will be identical to the foreign model—formally it will be quite different.

Application to Group Dynamics

These observations lead us to consider the insatiable desire of the foreigner to organize, to conquer, to instigate and to influence the people around him. On account of psychological difficulties, besides the barrier of the language, he is tempted to use the techniques of group dynamics he has learned and practiced in his own country. We can summarize the objectives of such "group dynamics" in the following way:

1 *development of insight* into the net of relationships, and consequently a better knowledge both of oneself and of the others;
2 *progress in the organization* of the group, or as the Western psychologists say, "interiorization" of the organization by the participants;

3 *personal change* due to awareness of the conditions and obstacles of
the successful working group.

What has been said already about the organization of Japanese society
should help in understanding the limited adequacy of these objectives in
Japan. Mention of insight immediately awakens suspicion. An insight,
literally, supposes a reflection of the individual upon oneself, namely a
movement which would originate in the individual and cut him off, at
least momentarily, from his group. The Japanese, however, participates
fully in the organization, and could not be more involved. One can almost
say that the group constitutes him, and not that he is the constituting
element. This effort which is required from a Japanese in the Western
context is contradictory to his linear sense of belonging, who by situation
cannot have a global concept of the group. As a link in the chain, he is
bound to the one above and the one below, that is all. He is a perfect link
insofar as he allows the vital energy to pass through himself without
interfering, without even noticing it.

Besides, this insight assumes in the Japanese the possibility of a purely
intellectual evaluation of his action. The differentiation between mental
activity and other activities (manual, voluntary, sensible or other) is
incompatible with the intense, total participation of the Japanese in every
act which almost suppresses all individuality except the acceptance of
playing such an anonymous role. This sudden independent step would
separate him from the group and render him unauthorized to express an
opinion about something of which he is no longer an active part. In other
words, to ask a Japanese to have an insight into the net of relationships is
to ask an artist to be conscious of his creative act. If the latter is obliged to
describe the process of his production, he is not an artist any more—he is
a theoretician of esthetics.

The second objective realized by "group dynamics" in the Western
sense is an "interiorization" of the organization. In Japan the organization exists before the individual, and almost "constitutes" the individual.
The being of the individual is the existence of the group. Is it possible to
dream of a deeper interiorization?

As far as personal change is concerned, the remarks made above have
sufficiently established that such a concept supposes the actuality of an
"ego" which would apprehend the other as "other." The Japanese are
living with the others and, consequently, are not "aware" of the conditions

and obstacles created by the group for the individual; they simply react to the concrete exigencies of action without theorizing about them.

After having shown that group dynamics in the Western sense are based upon the hypothesis of personal responsibility, however, it must be asserted that there is also a group dynamic in Japan, namely, the unconscious drive. This is the biological drive which will move the Japanese to adopt or to react to whatever could favor a fuller life, a better exchange inside and outside of the group. Thus, the substitution of one man for another, as in the case of foreign managers, implies in Japan that the newcomer must be not only the one who gives work and salary, but also the one who provides leisure, housing, amusement, welfare, retirement, and shows a real interest in the future of his personnel by helping not only their families, but also taking care of the various events in a man's life, such as weddings, births, sicknesses and even funerals. In other words, he must himself supply what is usually the responsibility of the community.

The Terms of Interrelationship

After having considered the interrelationships between the Japanese themselves, and between the Japanese and foreigners, let us examine the terms of this interrelationship.

In the same way as physical personality has to be considered rather as a relationship than as an independent unity, so the psychological ego should be interpreted not statistically but dynamically in relationship to the whole. In fact, only the whole has an ego—of course the branches of a tree have their singularity, but their real "ego" is the one of the tree—so much so that this life the Japanese are participating in can be said to be mine, yours and theirs at the same time. There are not two or several realities, but only a single one which can be considered from various sides. The Japanese seem to experience very strongly this absence of a real ego; they seem to exist by virtue of the whole, like the plant which although it lives through its roots, is thereby completely dependent upon its environment.

For foreigners, the ego is the meeting point of a system of relationships; for Japanese, the ego is the one relationship. The Westerners stress individuality; the Japanese stress the type, the role. If a pine could speak, it would not boast about being the tree which makes a corner of the landscape beautiful, but it would be flattered to be congratulated on being a pine. The plant bends to the sun in order to express more gloriously the splendor of its flowers; for this plant, strength consists of being weak, so that it is not only a product of its environment, but a compromise between the exterior forces and its inner self. The individual Japanese is the expression of society in its different manifestations; his ambition is not to be an outstanding Mr. Tanaka, but the perfect craftsman, the perfect salaryman, the perfect businessman; it is not his ambition, but only the efflorescence of Japan in one of its various functions.

It has become fashionable for Westerners to say that the Japanese do not have personalities. It is true that most of the Japanese leaders, at least the ones who are mentioned by the mass media, look and often are very dull. It is difficult to understand the rapid and splendid postwar recovery of Japan by looking at the faces of the executives. A little reflection on our own concept of personality, however, would help us understand that of the Japanese. There is a difference between personality and fame. If we ask ourselves why we consider de Gaulle and Kennedy personalities, it is not because one has a big nose and the other was good-looking, but because one somehow incarnates the determination of French tradition, and the other the vigor and energy of a strong country. They have given flesh and blood to two characteristics of their own people, and their individual personalities have almost been submerged under this expression. This illustration could give us a better insight of the Japanese personality.

Another consideration, this one historical, might be interesting. The Japanese have had personalities in the Western sense, and their biographies are now being published. Their disappearance at the beginning of this century may be explained by the ascendency of the militarists, who only allowed one to distinguish himself on the battlefield. Later, the necessity of making a living and coping with the necessities of life were not propitious to the formation of personalities, or the writing of biographies.

It looks as if the best way to explain Japanese psychology is through relationships, because everything is constituted or substantiated by its relationship to the whole, mainly in a vertical direction. The character of this relationship indicates the versatility of everybody and everything. Persons and things are used in Japan like pieces of a great puzzle. Diplomats become industry directors. Literature graduates are employed by security companies and banks, law graduates work as salesmen. All things concerning the owner are undetermined, because everything is common. The *furoshiki,* the traditional wrapping cloth, can be used for many purposes—it can protect all forms and all kinds of things. The *kimono* fits everyone—it is not patterned on the figure of its owner. *Geta* are made only in one size. The Japanese house can be transformed from a big room into several smaller ones by using light paper partitions. The bath *(ofuro)* is used by all the members of the family. The telephone, as well as the television set, is at the disposal of the whole neighborhood, as long as not everybody owns one.

Everything belongs to the group and the Japanese have very little regard for privacy or secrecy. Private deals are rather difficult in Japan. Everybody is informed about everything, and it costs very little to get accurate and detailed information about a whole family from special agencies. Details of bank accounts, properties, and less respectable items, can be and are known by everybody who is concerned with them. This has its advantages: as members of the group they are provided with all kinds of services. They are told repeatedly not to forget their belongings on the trains; they are led by a guide with a flag, in order to avoid the peril of being lost or not seeing whatever should be seen.

Should we conclude that the Japanese do not have any individuality? That is certainly not the opinion of the Japanese, who are convinced that they are, at least, very different from Westerners. Here precisely is the difference in point of view. The individuality of the Japanese consists of this unconscious or not rationally expressed rejection of an individuality in the Western sense. Strangely enough, Westerners complain about the absence in the Japanese of an evil which they regret, individualism.

According to this pattern of interrelationships, some human activities like authority, responsibility and decision-making take forms peculiar to Japan.

A *Authority and Responsibility*

We are accustomed to see authority concentrated in one man, who is

usually "outstanding" (the word in English evokes immediately a contradiction within Japanese society, where one should not "stand out.")
He is somebody, as we say, who knows his responsibilities; ironically
enough, we complain that too often the sense of responsibility is lost,
precisely because one person has subsumed the role of everybody. In
Japan, on the contrary, authority is delegated to one who "stands in"
rather than "out," and thus facilitates communication, or rather interchange, between all members of the group. Very often he has grown up
with the group, knows its members—or at least those of his own generation
who have greater responsibility—and has a talent, reinforced by training,
for keeping the exchange of communication flowing. There is a tendency
in Japan to reduce the role of a manager to a figurative one, even to an
ornament *(kazarimono)*. A Japanese social anthropologist points out
that the leader of, for example, an archeological expedition need not be
the most intelligent or the greatest scholar, but he must have been in the
field for a long time, so that he has experienced all the tensions proper to
that kind of activity, and has some kind of ability in dealing with them.
He is not chosen for his efficiency, but for the length of his acquaintance
with this or that kind of activity. He is the best channel for the irrigation
of all.

This modesty or refusal to make a decision comes from the sense of
solidarity which binds the Japanese together. The risk of ruining the
unity of thought and feelings of the group prevents one from taking over
the responsibility for all. The function of a leader is to anticipate (in the
sense of feeling according to a deep communion with all the others) the
expression of a desire (opinion or action), which is so essentially experienced by all that unanimity is already won before it is proposed.
This function is called *hara de wakaru* "to understand with the belly,"
another expression of this concrete way of getting acquainted with whom-
ever or whatever is around and on which the existence of everybody
and of the whole depends. Actually, authority and responsibility are
divided between all the members of the group: this distribution is
much easier because the carriers have gone through many selections to
become members, and already constitute a qualified elite. As a matter of
fact, there is no real authority, in our sense; there is only responsibility.
Authority would mean an individual direction, controlling or modifying
the development, but since the responsibility is not in any one person,

but in the group, there is no real authority, only a kind of mediatorship, a kind of harmonizing or feeling agent.

In fact, all authority comes from responsibility; responsibility comes from the task which has been assigned; and the assignment of the task comes from the general law of harmony which regulates the whole.

B *Decision-making*

This distribution of authority and responsibility is patterned according to the structure of the group: members, by growing in age and in experience, naturally assume more and more important roles.

The heavier tasks are assumed by the most experienced, but the most beautiful flower or the most succulent fruit can appear on the weakest sucker. Some suggestions may be made even by the youngest member of the group; throughout, seniors will assist in developing ideas proposed by other people. Indeed, in the proposal, the whole must be taken into account, especially the harmony and the equilibrium of the total body. There is an unwritten homeostatic law which imposes many precautions before any new element may be incorporated and integrated. The new element must somehow present a characteristic included specifically or generally in the nature of the activity of the group. Any coercion or forceful introduction is repugnant. The change or the modification requested by the new proposal will have to be "swallowed" and "digested" by the whole. Everybody will be informed about it (a move which often irritates the foreigner who is so careful of secrecy in his contacts), and the reaction or answer to the suggestion will slowly develop or mature through the whole body. At some point in the "digestion," a technical draft of the answer *(ringi-sho)* will be written by somebody who has experience in the specific field. Then the draft will go through the various sections of the organization where it will receive the seal *(han)* of the various responsible persons. Once all the seals have been affixed, the agreement will effectively have been made; there will be a decision. Let us carefully notice that the notion of majority did not come into account, because a suggestion contrary to the interest of the group would not have been made. On the contrary, a normal suggestion, one favorable to the organization, is ratified before it goes the round of seals. Consequently, there is no decision in our sense, obtained through reasoning, where somebody decides from above and his decision is ratified by counselors or members of the board. The word "decision" should be instead "confirmation"—confirmation of something which has already been vaguely approved by every member of the organization.

c Command

In this context, let us try to imagine the nature of a "command" in Japan. A command does not come from above in the sense of a direct and authoritarian intervention by the leader into the realm of another member of the group. Most of the time, it is a more accurate specification of the task according to the exigencies of the good functioning of the whole; it cannot be interpreted as a personal intervention of Mr. So-and-so. The command can be expressed through the means of a memo from the responsible person, which expresses, thus, the impersonal wish of the whole. The command cannot originate from outside, it must grow from inside, from some kind of pressure of discomfort eventually experienced by all. Life, to continue to flow through the organism, must be channeled properly and specifically; it is the command which solves the dilemma of the ambiguity. Every command must always look like some more efficient and conducive way of realizing harmony. In order that everyone may better fulfill his task, or in order that the various sections of the group may work more harmoniously, the general feeling and the universal consent of the personnel is that this correction be introduced, that this order be given. Those responsible for the specific section where the improvement is to be introduced confirm the unanimous wish by giving a command which is nothing but the clear expression of a vague impersonal wish.

If a foreign manager wants to give an order, he should start by talking with various levels of his personnel. If the suggestion is agreed upon by these people, usually after deliberating the "pros" and "cons," the order can be given according to the procedure of the *ringi-sho,* since everybody is in favor of it. It is interesting to note that the temptation of commanding, in the Western sense of the word, exists also among the Japanese. They call that type *tsuyoi hito,* the too individualistic man who does not take account of the group. You must have seen the expression of surprise and bewilderment on the face of the Japanese boilerman or Japanese laborer when a foreigner who is not his immediate superior speaks directly to him regarding his work. You tell him, for instance, that it is too warm in your office. He does not understand what you are talking about. He cannot see the relationship between your overheated office and his job as a boilerman. As far as he is concerned, his function has been determined by his immediate chief, and the coordinates of his responsibility have been given to him: he knows exactly where the needles of the various gauges should be when the boiler is on. That is his relationship to the general problem of heat, his task within the organization. The foreigner asks him to regulate the heat; that is not his problem, it is the problem of the supervisor. Let us go back to the fundamental idea of an organism. According to the general principle of adaptation and assimilation, the change wanted by the foreigner must also be wanted by the others, and chiefly by the one immediately responsible who will explain to the laborer the new or better conditions for fulfilling his task. Indeed, a man's task is determined not by his own will but by the exigencies of the proper functioning of the whole, which at every step will be translated by the man in charge. It could be said that the activity of the Japanese is not goal-directed, but fulfillment-directed. As we know already, the goal has been set up, and the only thing left is to achieve it in detail, according to the rules or forms.

A full explanation of the Japanese personality and of its various functions would require much more material and much longer study. Our present purpose will have been achieved if we have shown clearly that the vocabulary is confusing and that reality in the West and reality in Japan are by no means the same thing. Japan is not impenetrable, however; she requires only the utilization of the qualities of perception that our tradition and our rational training have left unemployed for many centuries, but which would make our life happier and fuller.

The Formation of an Industrial Society: Japan 1868–1914

by Robert J. Ballon

The Japanese economy today figures among the most developed economies of the world. The preceding article dealt with the Japanese development as an individual and as a group from the psychological and sociological angle. The second part of the "Background," the present study, is mainly empirical: it is an analysis of the formative years of the industrialization process.

Japan's history of industrialization began with the Meiji Reformation. The foundation for industrialization was in existence prior to the reformation; however, the necessary steps to move away from rural feudalism and into modern industrialism could not be taken until the nation as a whole "committed itself to industrialize". The first part deals with this commitment and studies its causes, its goals, its achievements. The commitment is analyzed as the mobilization of forces, how they were mobilized and to what end.

In the second part of the article, the author having established the motivation force, examines those who erected the economic monument and what respective roles the various organs played: the state, the industrialists and the labor force.

The author concludes by evaluating those primarily responsible for the success of industrialization.

THE FORMATION OF AN INDUSTRIAL SOCIETY: JAPAN 1868–1914

Commitment to Industrialization—The Artisans of Industrialization (The State, The Industrialists, The Labor Force)—Notes

Japan's economic tally is impressive, and many Western observers have taken pride in her unique position as the only industrialized nation outside the Western hemisphere, or—can one be that explicit?—in the fact that Japan was for many years the only Western-type nation outside the Western hemisphere! Even today the specific characteristics of Japan's industrialization are too easily considered as quaint ornaments of some "universal" phenomenon. Though a transistor may be "Made in Japan" or any other country for that matter, it does not follow that the process of industrialization was and is identical. The truth is that Japan is unique in having achieved an advanced degree of industrialization in a way that has no parallel in the West. Her achievements have equaled those of the West, but her industrial commitment was of a very different nature.[1]

Commitment to Industrialization

Japan never considered industrialization as an end in itself, or as the only means to enlarge the scope of opportunities open to the individual.[2] It was considered, from the start, as the indispensable tool whereby the nation could save its identity and accede to the rank of a modern power, on the same footing as the Western powers. Modernization had thereby as a goal to adopt what made other nations modern, and as a pattern to duplicate Western institutions. But the properly human aspect, namely the will to achieve modernization, was rooted in Japanese society.

For Japan, the commitment to industrialization meant, on the econ-

c

omic level: 1) importing technology in all its aspects; 2) building up the
needed overhead, primarily sea and rail transportation and communications; 3) creating the required capital. On the socio-political level, industrialization meant: 1) the abolition of the feudal system, for which a
centralized government and a national army were needed; 2) the abolition
of the hereditary class system by the free choice of occupation, and chiefly
by universal education; 3) the instauration of a money economy, obtained
by the conversion of the rice tax and the development of a banking system.

It is well known that the Meiji Restoration (1868) was not a Western-
type revolution from below; the masses had no say in the matter. The
new leaders of the nation felt that, in view of internal and international
circumstances, a new course was needed. Modernization was entered into
as a means of achieving not so much "traditional Japan without change,"
as "traditional Japan in a modern setting." A deep sense of national
emergency pervaded the entire venture: all energies were mobilized for
national survival.[3] This mobilization respected, however, the patterns
ingrained by the 250 years of the Tokugawa Shogunate: the cooperation
of all in a common task, but each in his place in the social hierarchy.

Pragmatic reforms succeeded one another, all dictated by the new
course. Universal conscription (1872) was required in order to preserve
national unity within the nation and amongst other nations. General
compulsory education (1872) was to develop and strengthen national
consciousness, while opening the minds of the people to "Civilization
and Enlightenment" (Bummei Kaika). Monetary reform (1871) and land
tax reform (1873) as well as the first national banks (1872) established the
money economy.

Industrialization proper was approached in exactly the same spirit.
In order to match the potential of "threatening" Western powers Japan
had to master their secret: industry. Industrialization did not result
from some emerging private initiative; it was, once and for all, a national
policy. Adequate measures were taken in rapid succession. No time or
resources were available to develop a capital market, but an elaborate
private banking system was fostered as a collector of savings and as the
source of capital funds. Little reliance was placed on foreign loans.
The foreign exchange needed to pay for the import of the tools of industrialization was provided by the sales of raw silk, tea, handicrafts, and so
on.

Lockwood has described the matter perfectly:

"The idea that the drive for foreign markets was *the* motor force of Japanese industrialization is nothing but a literary invention. . . The initial stimuli, and the new techniques, came largely from abroad. In this sense the Industrial Revolution in Japan was the creation of foreign trade. But the national response was positive and pervasive, working throughout the economy to produce changes which affected all sectors in varying degrees. It was precisely because this was so, and because it brought a steady rise in productivity and wealth, that imports and exports also grew."[4]

On the other hand, broad consensus on the part of the people at large is pointed out as an essential ingredient of successful industrialization in any country. Some state that Japan presented "an atypical pattern of little protest," and give as reason "the role of the old order in promoting industry and in constraining manifestations of worker protest through paternalistic enterprises and the State."[5] Much more was involved, however. Industrialization was a national policy, a common task, the task of everybody as a member of one or several of the many groups that form the nation, the national family in its totality. If consensus was obtained, it was as participation in a common undertaking, imposed on all and shared by all. The traditional value system proved most malleable in achieving what a scholar of the time, Sakuma Shōzan, expressed bluntly as "Eastern morality, Western techniques."

In the perspective of industrialization the basic social value of "devotion to the group" turned out to be most conducive to economic activity, once the "group" had been oriented toward rapid industrialization.

The Japanese finds himself coming into the world as a member of the group, to which he owes the very fact of his existence as well as his status in society.[6] Life—not "his" life—is a very practical reality: belonging to the group. Birth imposes a duty that can be expressed only by dedication to the group, and to its advancement; thereby the group repays itself and fulfils itself. The existence of the Japanese is the existence of the group itself, and it respects him as a member—not as an individual—on whom its existence depends.

The structure of the group is both vertical and horizontal. One always fulfils one's duty to it in an inferior position, in the sense that direction comes from above, and execution is achieved below; no superior is absolute, because there is always somebody else to whom he is inferior. On the horizontal plane, however, the direction given by the superior does not necessarily result from his better knowledge; it results rather from experience. Decision-making is thereby essentially a compromise between the forces at work within the group. The superior is not above the group.

The "group" is not just the family where physical birth takes place; the extended family, the industrial enterprise, various local communities, occupational and political organizations, etc., form a social fabric that, at its largest extent, covers the entire nation. Within this largest group, lower groups will overlap, and sectionalism is to be expected. But their final *raison d'être* is found in the nation, where a sense of permanency is obtained. Here take place the re-grouping of divergent pressures, the subordination of all particularism, the global implementation of the sense of duty.[7] In the West, the power of the state was steadily absorbed in an external, technical legal system. In Japan, national sovereignty was based on internal values, rather than on authority deriving from external laws. As a consequence, there has never been a clear demarcation line between public and private sectors.[8]

It is clearly understood that all groups achieve, in the final analysis, their collective survival and growth in the nation-state. Here is also where industrialization takes place. There is, therefore, little sense in the query of who influences whom, business or the government, implying what is commonly presupposed in the West, a gap between business and the government; in Japan, they are rather the two sides of the same coin. One side is definitely not the other, but both combine to produce the given reality of Japan's industrialization.

The Artisans of Industrialization

A *The State*

Since the West had developed its industries along capitalistic lines, the Meiji government followed suit. It would soon call on private industrialists to play an active role, but first the proper social and economic climate had to be created. No pains were spared in the often tricky task of fanning interest in the new ways. The slogan "Civilization and Enlightenment" *(Bummei Kaika),* meant that Japan would survive as Japan, and thus prove her superiority over threatening nations by adopting many of their ways. Universal education, in fact, would bring Japan in less than two generations among the countries with the highest rate of literacy, an achievement all the more essential since "Western arts" were imported chiefly by books and publications, which themselves had first to be translated into an idiom not traditionally suited.[9] Transportation became a spearhead of development: during several years one-third of total government investments went into railways; an average of 1.5 million passengers per year traveled on the newly opened Tokyo-Yokohama line; and by 1868, Japan had already well over 100 modern ships, mostly purchased abroad. Monetary problems were tackled in earnest. Up until 1874, for example, foreign trade was almost entirely in the hands of foreign companies, and specie was flowing out at a rapid rate; the banking system was expanded, in 1876, by a new banking law, and private banks started to mushroom.

At the outset it was imperative to show potential private industrialists the techniques of industry. The government played the role of initiator: model enterprises were launched under state sponsorship. The quickest way, but an expensive one, was of course to import production processes *in toto:* raw materials, machinery, lay-out, engineers and technicians.[10] At the same time, Western methods of business administration were introduced, and joint-stock companies were launched on a grand scale.[11] On the other hand, many Japanese visited the West to study how to manage enterprises. The number of students sent abroad as of 1872 totalled 373, of whom 250 were maintained at government expense.[12] In 1870, the Ministry of Industry *(Kobu-sho)* was established where most of these activities were coordinated.

By the early 1880s, the stage had been set. The best part of state-managed enterprises, with the exception of armament and related industries, began to be sold to private entrepreneurs on terms very favorable to the latter. From this point on, the government would essentially limit itself to the role of promoter by encouraging industrial development and protecting it in all possible ways, especially by being its chief customer during the critical years prior to 1895, when the internal demand for many industrial goods had had no time as yet to build up.[13]

The men most directly engaged in the government sponsorship of industrialization were former members of the samurai class from South-Western Japan. They had acquired under the Tokugawa regime a keen sense of public administration based on loyalty to their feudal lords. When these lords succeeded in overthrowing the Tokugawa, their retainers were entrusted with the execution of the new course. Out of their ranks came some of the private industrialists who would step forward after 1880. From then on, government bureaucracy never failed in its strong conviction that national independence requires industrialization, that industrialization requires active governmental cooperation.

"These early bureaucrats had in common a respect for Western learning which most of them had studied, and a lively sense of the need to convert Japan into a rich and powerful state.

The major steps in their program for the building of such a rich and powerful state included the abolition of the feudal system, hereditary servitude, and restraints on travel and choice of occupation; the consolidation of local, provincial, and national governments and their monetary functions; and the establishment of universal education and military conscription. These reforms were without exception planned and carried out by these early modern bureaucrats."[14]

The bureaucracy introduced the Commercial Code in 1889, and devised a tax system meant as an incentive for industrial corporations. Some practices may be questioned, like the very common one of giving government contracts without recourse to public competitive bidding to monopoly contractors called "merchant contractors under government patronage" *(Goyō shōnin)*. It appears that monopoly profits were not frowned upon, so long as these profits were by and large reinvested. It is well known that the main government contractors were usually the most enterprising industrialists. At any rate, government bureaucracy stood by as one man, while never losing sight of the task to be done in the greatest hurry: to industrialize!

"The role of the government as a supporter of modern ventures was very important indeed. But it was the indirect subsidies that were of first consequence: the government trading contracts, the depositing of official funds without interest, the low-interest long-term loans, monopolies, tax incentives, and the like. These took the place of tariff protection which is usually necessary to shield young industries in latecomer countries. But while tariff protection across the board helps all firms in an industry, whether they are efficient or not, the Meiji government could pick its favorites on the basis of ability, which means on the basis of success. Those which received more and grew into giants, and were run by seasoned entrepreneurs who worked with a passion for money, for personal power, and for the country. Indirect subsidies of this kind, avoiding the inefficiencies of both tariff protection and government operations, promoted a concentration of capital that had far-reaching effects on the entire course of Japanese economic development."[15]

Until 1945, the state never felt much need for social policies to cope with the social impact of industrialization, because these were matters falling within the realm of the family system and employer paternalism. It should be pointed out, however, that during the period before the military regime, the bureaucracy did draft certain elaborate and comprehensive labor laws. This came about as a result of the accusation of social dumping made abroad, but the parliament subsequently watered down these drafts.

B   *The Industrialists*

By the 1880s, Japanese society had achieved a certain stability, and forceful industrialization now required a type of man with a sense of business administration and capital accumulation; it seems that this indispensable human resource could be found among samurai and commoners.[16] The leading entrepreneurs, who took the reins of industrialization from the hands of the State, were either former samurai willing to leave their positions with the government (because this new job was but the further implementation of the national policy), or "outsiders" who had become convinced that, by now, the risk was worth the game. Over the centuries of the Tokugawa regime, the merchant class had grown slowly in importance, as the feudal lords ran deeper and deeper into financial troubles and came to depend on the merchants for their finances.[17] An astute sense for business had thereby been developed. A number of leading merchants, some of samurai origin, established prosperous family trading enterprises where capital accumulation was inculcated on moral grounds also. All the members of the house *(ie)* were expected to economize by virtue of family rules; profits were not allotted to them, but to the family. These rules of conduct, perfect examples of traditional samurai spirit, if it had not been for the use of money, were later applied to the management of industrial enterprises.[18] One of the entrepreneurial slogans of the time was: "The spirit of the samurai combined with the ability of the merchant" *(Shikon-shosai)*.

This is the reason why entrepreneurship, even in the case of some single-handed and strong-minded industrialists, always remained group-centered; it was an expected contribution from and to the group, in the final instance, the nation, rather than an expression of pioneering individualism. Contrary to the Western captains of industry seeking their own profit and achieving industrialization almost against the will of the masses, Japanese industralists have always felt entrusted with a "national mission." Their function has been to protect the commonweal against the internal threat of the paucity of indigenous resources and the pressure of population,[19] of raw materials, and international competition. They shared industrialization with government, in its economic aspects (foreign trade, industrial commitment, etc.) as well as in its social aspects (paternalism and employment policies), to the extent that distinction between the public sector and the private one would easily be obliterated.[20] The overriding purpose of starting an industrial venture was not so much to make profits, though they were substantial and as substantially reinvested, nor personal aggrandizement, though fame was bestowed and gleefully appreciated, as to fulfil the role of an agent of the national policy of industrialization. Industrialists, or the government for that matter, never claimed a monopoly over, or the credit for the *Bummei Kaika*. It belonged to Japan.

c *The Labor Force*

Arnold Toynbee speaks of the "creative minority," and the Inter-University Study Group of the "industrializing elite," and one can easily picture the rugged individualists in the West who launched the process of industrialization without much support, if any, from the government and the masses. In Japan, however, not merely a passive, but a very active response of the people has been a factor of industrialization. But it follows that the industrial labor force could not develop in an autonomous way and would remain strapped by the global web of rules of society.

During the Tokugawa period, the farmers were referred to as the "pillars of the nation," because they provided the ruling military class with its mainstay, the rice tax. The same farmers now became the foundation on which the national policy of industrialization could rest. They provided 1) needed manpower; 2) foreign exchange by the export of their products, raw silk, tea, and handicrafts; 3) domestic savings, channelled through the banking system as the main source for investment funds; 4) a rapidly increasing agricultural productivity that almost kept up with the increasing population. A psychological distance between rural and industrial life never really developed because through the family system, up until the 1930s, close ties with the rural family were kept alive to the extent that in case of unemployment the industrial worker could always go back to the countryside.[21] But much more important was the psychological effect of keeping the communication channels between rural and industrial workforces wide open: the traditional qualities of the farmers, thrift, diligence and patience, flowed unhampered into the bloodstream of industrialization.

> "The complex system of terraces, irrigation, sub-soil and so on, required years of work by a whole family or village. They represented a major capital investment, and a young man with initiative was a man who knew how to show patience with his elders until that investment came into his hands."[22]

The commitment to industrial employment, consequently, took roots progressively and, all in all, quite smoothly, because it never made a frontal attack on the traditional fabric of society.

Until World War I, industrial workers consisted largely of transient workers drawn from rural areas, and were without much industrial specificity, in small proportion to the total labor force. Since the stable part of the urban population was mainly active in tertiary industries, the bulk of the industrial labor force had to come from the rural districts. It was composed overwhelmingly of the human resource not immediately needed for agricultural production: the young female worker. As late as 1930, half of the industrial labor force was female, employed chiefly in the textile industry, and would not remain in industrial employment for much more than five years.

In the first decades of her industrialization, Japan knew, therefore, great difficulties, not in obtaining a universal consensus to the new course, but in successfully committing her labor force to industrial employment. Many practices, often of a paternalistic nature, were developed by the modern industries, such as in-plant training, factory dormitories, welfare programs, deferred payment of wages, etc.[23] The problem found its natural solution with the industrial expansion at the time of World War I, but industrial employment had been marked indelibly with traits that would, a generation later, bunch into the institution of lifelong employment.

Who is responsible for Japan's industrialization? The names of famous industrialists of the Meiji era are given: Shibusawa Eiichi, the president of the Dai-ichi Bank and founder of Hitotsubashi University; Iwasaki Yatarō, the builder of the Mitsubishi empire; Minomura Rizaemon, the head clerk of the House of Mitsui, and Masuda Takashi, the founder of the Mitsui Trading Company; Hirose Saihei, whose interest in copper was the basis on which was built the Sumitomo concern; Yasuda Zenjirō, the banker; and many more. It is a characteristic of Western terminology and way of thinking to select these individuals as the entrepreneurs of Meiji Japan.[24] These men however would not have come forth without the active support of such government officials as Inoue Kaoru, Ohkubo Toshimichi, or Ohkuma Shigenobu, military men such as Yamagata Aritomo, or Oyama Iwao, and without the untiring efforts of scholars such as Yoshida Shōin, whose disciples were the leaders of the Restoration party, and Fukuzawa Yukichi, whose students staffed among others Mitsubishi and Mitsui, and who founded Keiō University.

But these men, though their contribution was vital, were not the real determinant of Japan's industrialization. Japan's entrepreneur was her people, powerfully knit together by a boundless ambition to show the world that they could achieve industrialization quickly and successfully. The resilience of the Japanese economy, so eloquently proven over one century, comes precisely from the fact that industrialization was from the very beginning more than the sum, with all the inner conflicts, of divergent interests. Industrialization was part and parcel of the structure of Japanese sociey, of the spirit of the nation, of its will to succeed.

¹ This article is a slightly revised portion of a paper presented at the International Labor Relations Conference, sponsored by the Japan Institute of Labor, Tokyo, February 1–5, 1965 and published in *Changing Problems of Industrial Relations,* Tokyo, The Japan Institute of Labor, 1965, pp. 30–54.

² The development of the internal consumer market would have to wait until after World War II. See to the contrary: Alan H. Gleason, "Economic Growth and Consumption in Japan," in William W. Lockwood (ed.), *The State and Economic Enterprise in Japan,* Princeton, Princeton University Press, 1965, pp. 391 ff.

³ The term "national emergency" as used here refers to what Western nations have experienced too often in time of war: a total mobilization of all the nation's energies. Fervent advocates of economic liberalism do not hesitate, then, to call for what in peace time would be branded as outright government interference!

⁴ William W. Lockwood, *The Economic Development of Japan: Growth and Structural Change, 1868–1938,* Princeton: Princeton University Press, 1954, p. 309. See concurrence by Henry Rosovsky, *Capital Formation in Japan, 1868–1940,* The Free Press of Glencoe, 1961, pp. 95–97.

⁵ Clark Kerr *et al., Industrialism and Industrial Man,* London, Heinemann, 1962, p. 209.

⁶ In the West, an individual may join a group and devote himself totally to the group, by some decision of his individual will. This is not the case in Japan: the Japanese is not born as an "individual," but is constitutively a member of the group.

⁷ The Western concept of "nationalism" applied here would be misleading. In Japan, nationalism never swelled into a movement of popular emancipation: popular uprisings were quelled in the name of national unity. Geographical and historical circumstances have powerfully reinforced this consciousness of the national, ethnocentric group.

⁸ See Masao Maruyama, *Thought and Behaviour in Modern Japanese Politics,* Oxford University Press, 1963, p. 7. And the same author quotes a war-time text: "What we normally refer to as 'private life' is, in the final analysis, the way of the subject. As such it has a public significance, in that each so-called private action is carried out by the subject as part of his humble efforts to assist the Throne. . . Thus we must never forget that even in our personal lives we are joined to the Emperor and must be moved by the desire to serve our country." (Ministry of Education, *Shimmin no Michi* (The Way of the Subject), 1941).

⁹ The percentage of children of compulsory school age enrolled increased from 28.13 percent in 1873, to 48.93 in 1890, and 98.14 percent in 1910; from 1920 on, the percentage stayed above 99. (Ministry of Education, *Japan's Growth and Education,* Tokyo, 1963, p. 160).

¹⁰ It is interesting to note that it was Japan's national unity that protected her from getting swamped in this technical dependence, that lessened, however, as years went by. H. Rosovsky makes an interesting distinction between technology in the physical sense and technology in the "spiritual" sense *(Op. cit.,* pp. 91–104.) Between 1870 and 1885, the Ministry of Industry employed over 500 foreign engineers and technical

instructors, of whom a vast majority was British (See Tuge Hideomi, *Historical Development of Science and Technology in Japan,* Tokyo, 1961, p. 97.)

[11] In 1874, the Ministry of Finance established its own school with a four-year course in banking, finance, and book-keeping (See Johannes Hirschmeier, *The Origins of Entrepreneurship in Meiji Japan,* Cambridge, Harvard University Press, 1964, p. 128.) In 1878, destitute samurai, a considerable headache for the Meiji leaders, their former peers, were offered government loans to start joint-stock ventures with samurai as members.

[12] See Kazuo Noda, "The Entrepreneurship in the Early Meiji Period," *Quarterly Review of Management,* Tokyo, January-March 1964, p. 29. Also Hirschmeier, *op. cit.,* pp. 122–123.

[13] See Hirschmeier, *ibid.,* p. 153. The nationalization of the railways, main trunk-lines in the late 1900s was one of those exceptions confirming the rule.

[14] Masamichi Inoki, "The Civil Bureaucracy. A. Japan," in Robert E. Ward and Dankwart A. Rustow (eds), *Political Modernization in Japan and Turkey,* Princeton, N.J., Princeton University Press, 1964, p. 289.

[15] Hirschmeier, *op. cit.,* p. 241.

[16] Japanese scholars, before World War II, stressed heavily the role played by the samurai; in recent years, growing credit is given to the merchant class as such. Both interpretations seem to be greatly determined by the atmosphere of the time at which they are made.

[17] In this respect, the fact that merchants were considered as "parasites" of the feudal society was of some help to them. The full burden of the taxes was carried by the farmers; but merchants would, every so often, be forced to write off their loans to the lords. (See Charles David Sheldon, *The Rise of the Merchant Class in Tokugawa Japan, 1600–1868,* New York, J.J. Augustin, 1958.) Many old established merchant houses collapsed in the early years after the Restoration, when the debts of a great number of large feudal lords were nullified by the new government. (See Hirschmeier, *op. cit.,* p. 30.)

[18] The rules of the Iwasaki House, a family of samurai origin and founder of the Mitsubishi concern, are typical:

1 Do not take up small projects, but aim at the management of large enterprises.
2 Once you start an enterprise, be sure to succeed in it.
3 Do not engage in speculative enterprises.
4 Operate all enterprises with the national interest in mind.
5 Never forget the pure spirit of public service and righteousness.
6 Be hard-working and frugal, and thoughtful to others
7 Utilize qualified personnel.
8 Treat your employees well.
9 Be bold in starting an enterprise, but meticulous in its prosecution.

(Iwai Ryōtarō, *Mitsubishi Concern Tokuhon* (The Mitsubishi Concern Reader), Tokyo, 1937, p. 238.) A growing number of Japanese scholars compare this contribution of tradition to the role attributed by Max Weber to the Protestant Ethic in Western industrialization.

[19] Still a few years ago, many Japanese managers would justify what to foreigners appears as a redundance of manpower, by stating their obligation to provide employment to as many people as possible.

[20] "For the logic according to which 'private affairs' cannot be morally justified within themselves, but must always be identified with national affairs, has a converse implication: private interests endlessly infiltrate national concerns." (Maruyama, *op. cit.*, p. 7.)

[21] Unemployment compensation was not enacted before 1947.

[22] Richard K. Beardsley, John W. Hall and Robert E. Ward, *Village Japan*, pp. 476-477.

[23] See Makoto Sakurabayashi and Robert J. Ballon, "Labor-Management Relations in Modern Japan: A Historical Survey of Personnel Administration," in Joseph Roggendorf (ed.), *Studies in Japanese Culture: Tradition and Experiment*, Tokyo, Sophia University, 1963, pp. 244-266.

[24] As does, e.g. Hirschmeier, *op. cit.*

Part Two
THE ECONOMY

IN PART I, *the background has been set forth, and now we move into the reality of today.*

In this article, the author brings up to date the Japanese economic scene of the 1960's. The article does not attempt to give an explanation of the post-war economic miracle, which is familiar to all, but it analyzes the actual measures taken to try to keep the Japanese economy on the strait path—avoiding the pitfalls of both inflation and recession. The main problem here is the rather paradoxical situation that whereas some desperately warned that the economy was heading straight for an inflation, others just as vociferously warned of an impending depression. Many sound and well established macro-economic policies failed; the question is why.

The anti-cyclical measures taken in the years from 1960 to 1965, and the effects of these measures are pointed out within the context of the development of the economy.

Finally, the author ascribes the reason for this paradoxical situation of simultaneous inflation and deflation to the complexity of the economic structures in Japan. He concludes that the structures of the economy are the principal barrier to improvement; and that although the anti-cyclical measures which were taken are sound theoretically, they are nevertheless futile as long as those "anti-economic structures" persist.

CHAPTER III

Japan's Economic Situation

by Jose M. Abad

From the point of view of the science and art of economic policy, the latter years of Japan's economic life (1961–65) represent an odd phenomenon, which challenged both policy-makers as well as scholars.

This challenge does not arise from the speed of Japan's economic growth, which, amazing and complicated as it is, has been properly analyzed and sufficiently understood.

The challenge for the policy-maker and for the scholar rather centers around the following major facts:

1 Many macro-economic measures, which have been recently adopted as sound and established economic policy, failed alarmingly. Why?

2 There has been in the last years a surprising clash of opinion among the different leaders (businessmen, politicians, scholars) in contact with the economic life of the country.

Some of them claimed the Japanese economy was under a strong and persistent inflationary trend and consequently asked for monetary measures to be taken. Others pointed out that a recession mood was sweeping everything and that strong symptoms of depression had already begun to appear.

Who were (and are) right? Those claiming that Japan is experiencing an inflation, or those claiming a depression.

JAPAN'S ECONOMIC SITUATION

*Inflation? Recession?—Standard Anti-cyclical Measures—
Economic Structure (Capital, Labor Mobility and Productivity,
Market Distribution)—Conclusion.*

In macro-economic terms it sounds contradictory to say that a specific
economy finds itself under both inflation and depression at the same time.

The Japanese arguing that Japan suffers from inflation appeal to the
standard definition of inflation: "A process of rising prices (not merely
high prices)." Inflation is certainly a disequilibrium situation. By merely
looking at the external phenomenon of rising prices, inflation is obvious.
Government authorities took it for granted that this inflation arose from
"normal" sources, like demand inflation (as expressed by Keynes and
Wicksell). Even during periods when a tight money policy was clearly
adopted, overall consumer prices, especially foodstuffs, rose impressively.

From 1959 to 1960, foodstuff consumer prices rose 4.7%. They kept
going up and, from 1960 to 1961, rose by 6.7%. A peak was reached
during 1962, when they increased by 8.2%. There was a small check
during 1963 (7.2% increase only), and then an all-out effort was made
to check this price rise during 1964–65. For a short time it looked as if it
could be controlled, but soon, during the second half of 1964, prices
increased again by 8.4%. The independence shown by foodstuff prices,
disregarding the tight money policy, fostered the idea that Japan was suf-
fering from a severe inflationary trend.

Personal services also contributed to the rise in consumer prices.
They showed a total increase of 57.2% in the years 1960–64, and maintained the trend till the late summer of 1965.

When analyzing the reasons for this inflation and inflationary trend,
one well established opinion summarizes the causes of inflation as follows:

1 There has been a low increase in the production of foodstuffs, per-

sonal services and other areas showing inflation; consequently the increase in supply did not match the step-up in consumer demand occasioned by the increase in non-corporate and personal income.

2   A standard overheating of the economy took place and the standard spiral of wages-prices-wages appeared.

These and other similar causes, which are considered standard causes of inflation, have obviously played their role in the Japanese inflationary trends: in general any wage hike tends to reflect itself in the rise of prices in areas where productivity does not improve, or improves at a rate below the average. Pure theory would require a situation of full employment as the condition for this type of inflation. As a matter of fact, inflation appears even without full employment. The typical case presented by the Economic Planning Agency refers to the relationship between the rate of personnel expenses and the increase in charges for services: the higher the personnel expenses ratio in the total amount of expenditures, the higher the rate of service charges: education tuition, personal services (barber, tailor, laundry, etc.), drinking water, transportation, mail, telephone, electricity, gas, television, radio and so on.

Here are two examples of increases in service prices: haircut: 18% in 1962, 18% in 1963, 12.2% in 1964, 12.2% in 1965; average rent for a house: 9.1% in 1963, 10.5% in 1964.

Certainly the most apparent and easy-to-understand factor causing the price increase has been expanding demand. Equipment and inventory investments by private corporations alone induced an increase in Japan's GNP of 6 to 7 percent annually, during the last seven years. But, since the latter part of 1960, private consumption expenditures began to increase at an annual rate of 12 to 13 percent.

Japan's economy is getting closer to the stage of economic development where private and public consumption become as important prime movers of economic growth as capital investment. Already rising consumer prices and the growth in the marginal propensity to consume tend to increase wage costs and to weaken the competitive strength of Japanese industries on the world market.

Rate of rise in some consumer prices
(1960–64)

	(percentage)
Overall	25.6%
Foodstuffs	28.8
cereals	18
fresh fish	52
milk & eggs	10
vegetables	59
grocery	41
processed food	45
confectionary	28
fruits	52
beverages	21
Housing	22.2
house & land rents	45
house repairing	36
drinking water charge	21
Light & fuel	7.6
Clothing	19.2
Incidentals	28.0
medical & sanitary expenses	21
transportation & communication	17
education	53
culture & entertainment	35

Source: *Consumer Price Index, Tokyo*, Bureau of Statistics, Office of the Prime Minister.

Recession?

In spite of these trends, which unquestionably appeared as inflationary, there has been, especially since October 1964, a simultaneous trend of deflation and even depression in the macro-economic dimension. Already during the first half of 1964, symptoms of macro-economic recession were at hand, mainly the continuous bankruptcies of medium and small enterprises. Although these bankruptcies constituted a normal phenomenon of the Japanese economy, the giant scale of 1964's bank-ruptcies indicated a period of recession, after the Government's tight-money policy was imposed.

In December 1964, 596 businesses, with liabilities totaling ¥93,000 million, failed; this was a 15% increase over the previous month. The total number of bankruptcies in 1964, 4,212 businesses, with liabilities totaling ¥463,100 million, surpassed that of the previous record year of 1962.

The most noted bankrupt companies were Nihon Tokushukō with a capital of ¥3,090 million, and Sunwave Kōgyō with a capital of ¥2,825 million. In a chain reaction, quite a number of other bankruptcies re-sulted. Per-bankruptcy liabilities rose from ¥114,000,000 in November to ¥156,000,000 in December. The biggest case was that of Sanyō Tokushukō. 1965 witnessed even more bankruptcies.

The Government again faces a dilemma: to help these small and me-dium industries, or to leave them to their fate.

A discrepancy manifested itself among those maintaining that Japan was under recession: it was said that only the micro-economic world, not the macro-economic world, was in recession and that the divergence between micro- and macro-economics could be considered normal in a period of readjustment. Therefore, Japan was facing, they said, a normal cyclical crisis of recession. Any doubts about Japan's economy being in recession lost ground during October-December 1964: Japan's GNP stopped its increase, and even began to decline around March-April of 1965. Almost the same could be said about personal consumption ex-penditure, private equipment investment, and inventory investment.

Standard anti-cyclical measures

Japanese policy-makers dealt successively with both the inflationary and deflationary trends, applying standard countermeasures of anticy-clical nature; some anti-inflationary, others anti-deflationary; sometimes contradictory measures were taken simultaneously.

A glance at six years of the Japanese economy shows how standard economic measures were taken to check inflationary trends.

1960

The expansion of the economy continued in 1960 (real growth of GNP of fiscal 1960 over fiscal 1959: 11.0%). Until the middle of the year, the Bank of Japan held its line of checking sudden expansion of the money supply and stressing preventive policies. But with the installation of the Ikeda cabinet, monetary policy underwent a drastic change. Ikeda's fundamental policies were:

1 an ample supply of funds to make a high rate of economic growth possible;

2 lowering of money rates to reduce capital costs of enterprises and to improve their competitive position in world markets.

The bankers had envisaged lower interest rates as the effect of improved monetary elasticity; Ikeda considered them as a means of implementing his short-term objectives. Consequently, the Ministry of Finance urged the city banks to lower their interest rates on deposits. On January 25, 1961, the official discount rate was lowered to 1.8 sen (6.57% p.a.), and on April 1, a general reduction of interest rates was effected. The rate of interest on postal savings was lowered to 5% on six-month time deposits and 5.5% on one-year time deposits, while the rate of interest on current deposits was set at 3.6%. The interest rates paid by the banks on time deposits were set at 4% for three months, 5% for six months, and 5.5% for one year. Rates on demand deposits were lowered by 0.1% sen p.d. Interest rates on trust deposits for two years were lowered by 0.5% to 6.3%, and those for five years by 0.43% to 7.07%; those on loan trusts were reduced to 6.3% and 7.37%, for two- and five-year trusts, respectively. Yields on government bonds remained unchanged (long-term obligations, 6.432%, short-term bonds, 6.023%). But returns on new debentured issues were lowered. The interest rate on long-term loans by the Industrial Bank or the Long-Term Credit Bank to electric power companies was reduced from 9.125% to 8.7%.

The main point here is that despite the official policy of monetary relaxation, the call market remained very tight throughout 1960. After a period of relative calmness at the beginning of 1961, the demand for funds, not only on the part of city banks but also by securities companies, increased sharply. Insurance companies, mutual banks and credit co-operatives were the chief suppliers of these funds.

1961

The large deficits on current account in the balance of payments at the beginning of 1961 caused anxiety in some circles over the direction of the economy. By June, the view that the investment fever was running too high and that an adjustment was necessary was universally accepted.

Measures:

In July, the official discount rate was raised by 0.1 sen (1.9 sen p.d.) (6.935%); the discount rate for export bills was reduced to 1.2 sen p.d. (4.38% p.a.), the lowest since 1948.

In September, the official discount rate was 2 sen (7.3%). The reserve ratio of the banks was increased. Interest rates on bank deposits and long-term loans were not raised, so that the difference between long-term and short-term loans widened and the bond market became less active.

Effects:

The tight-money policy failed to slow down the economy immediately and it was only later that its effects were actually felt. But fund demand remained very pressing because industry, instead of financing new investments, now found it necessary to finance large inventories, despite drastic cutbacks in production and a severe curtailment of operating rates.

The enforcement of the tight-money policy was tempered by some measures designed to relieve the distress caused by the deflation. In particular, efforts were made to prop up the sagging stock market. The Ministry of Finance increased the ceiling on new investment trusts to be set up by security companies, allowing each firm a net increase of ¥20 billion instead of the former ¥18 billion. It also removed the ¥9 billion limitation on investments in call loans and bonds, so that these transactions were no longer held down to a certain limit. For the same purpose of bolstering sagging stock prices, the Securities Finance Company raised the ceiling on some of its credits while the regulations for credit transactions on the securities market were relaxed.

The banks found it increasingly difficult to satisfy the pressing fund demand of industry out of their own resources. Central bank credit made up the deficiency, and the situation became exceedingly tight in 1961 when, despite the various credit controls, borrowing from the Bank of Japan increased by one and a half times over the preceding year. In

February of 1962, loans and discounts of the Bank of Japan actually exceeded the note issue.

1962

The balance of payments regained equilibrium in June 1962, and in October some steps were taken to relax the monetary stringency. The official discount rate was lowered by 0.1 sen, and the punitive rates on bank borrowings from the central bank were reduced to 0.3 sen.

The ratio of reserve requirements was also lowered, effective November 1. For banks with deposits over ¥100 billion, the reserve ratio was 0.5% for time deposits.

In November 1962, the Bank of Japan again lowered the discount rate by 0.1 sen (1.8 sen; 6.57% p.a.). At the same time, the Bank of Japan decided to regulate the future money supply by open-market operations. Up to then, additional currency was supplied almost exclusively through advances by the central bank to city banks, so that an expansion in the circulation of bank notes coincided with increased bank borrowings.

Bank of Japan Official Rates

Year and Month	Commercial bills discount (sen) (per diem per ¥100)	Loans on security of national bonds (sen)
1959 Feb.	1.9	2.0 & up
Dec.	2.0	2.1 ,,
1960 Aug.	1.9	2.0 ,,
1961 Jan.	1.8	1.9 ,,
July	1.9	2.0 ,,
Sept.	2.0	2.1 ,,
1962 Oct.	1.9	2.0 ,,
Nov.	1.8	1.9 ,,
1963 Mar.	1.7	1.8 ,,
Apr.	1.6	1.7 ,,

Source: Bank of Japan

1963–64

The government again resumed its drive for cheap money and, in quick succession, the official discount rate was lowered twice—on March 19, 1963, and on April 19, by 0.1 sen each time, so that the rate came down to 1.7 sen p.d. (6.205% p.a.), the lowest since 1955. The rate on export trade bills was reduced to 1.1 sen p.d. (4.015% p.a.).

In order to prevent its low-interest policy from unduly inflating credit and worsening the already precarious capital structure of industrial enterprises, the government proposed application of the so-called "World Bank formula" to domestic bank credit. The plan foresaw fixing a certain standard for the ratio of liabilities to internal capital and the liquidity ratio (ratio of short-term liabilities to liquid assets). In this way, enterprises would be forced to increase their own capital and banks would be stopped from granting new loans to heavily indebted companies. The government hoped to rectify the "overloan" situation of the large banks and reduce the ratio of loans to deposits to 85:100 in the next five years.

1965

This was an illuminating year for policy-makers. The standard "easy money" measures were not enough for an adequate recovery of business. The Economic Policy Council, in July 1965, decided to acknowledge that:

a) A recession was widely established, and a danger of serious depression had appeared.

b) Extra fiscal measures (not merely monetary) would be needed.

These extra measures were:

1 To accelerate expenditures for public works up to the end of 1965 by about ¥100 billion.

2 To advance fiscal investments amounting to about ¥120 billion to the July-September quarter.

3 To speed up the issuing of local public bonds amounting to ¥10 billion.

4 To increase fiscal investments by about ¥210 billion.

5 To reduce the standard interest rate of the government's financial institutions for small enterprises (Small Business Finance Corporation, People's Finance Corporation, Central Bank for Com-

mercial and Industrial Cooperatives) by 0.3% p.a. (effective September 1).

6 To strengthen measures for promoting exports.

7 To keep consumer prices down (to postpone raises in the rates of public utilities, to take the necessary budgetary measures for stabilizing commodity prices).

8 To effect a long-range tax reduction.

9 To provide for fiscal revenues by the flotation of government bonds.

These measures were again standard anticyclical measures in themselves, which are normally more efficient in creating and expanding effective demand than the pure monetary measures. But still, the problem remains: are these measures (monetary and fiscal alike) enough to cope with a cycle, whose root lies perhaps in the wrong economic structures of the country? Unfortunately, not even these drastic fiscal measures have helped as much as required.

Economic Structure

The main question to be answered is why these standard measures did not produce the results which they normally do in similar cases.

The anti-inflationary measures did not stop the price spiral, nor did the anti-deflationary measures induce a recovery. The reason is that these measures are supposed to work fully only when applied to a standard case of inflation or deflation. I consider a standard case here to be the inflation or deflation which arises from a conjunctural situation. Inflation may come from a cost push or from an overheating of demand, or an overheating of demand-supply. Deflation may appear because of over-investment or over-saving. These would constitute the standard conjunctural cases.

In Japan, besides the conjunctural cycle, a deeper factor has contributed in a decisive way to the successive inflation and deflation—the complex of economic structures. These peculiar structures have, in part, artificially forced and set up an inflation and a deflation process.

For a better understanding of the issue, let us recall that the fundamental aim of a free economy is to secure through the market mechanism (supply and demand) the best (re-)allocation of resources (labor force, capital, material resources) and the best rationality in production (least cost, best profit). In some instances, of course, a limitation of the free economy is necessary, especially in income distribution (e.g. wages), or for other resources or products, in order to satisfy other claims (e.g. social justice).

But in a free economy, the elements extrinsic to the market mechanism (e.g. State interventionism) which set the framework of competition should not in principle interfere directly with the free play of demand and supply. The equilibrium between demand and supply in a centralized economy is supposed to come from central planning and compulsory execution; in a free economy, it is expected from the elasticity of demand and supply, investment (private and public), and periods of adjustment.

In Japan, the following structures have unduly affected this economic mechanism and provoked a conjunctural cycle, which cannot be efficiently checked by mere standard anti-cyclical measures:

1 Capital and credit.
2 Lack of labor mobility and lack of productivity increase.
3 Market distribution.

A *Capital*

1 In spite of the tremendous (marginal) propensity to save the money supply newly created in 1961, spending exceeded private savings by over ¥1,000 billion. This fact is only a symptom of the admitted need for capital. Since budgeting and positive balance of payments are not "practiced" in Japan, the commercial bank's bills and some advances by the Bank of Japan are the only real way of creating money.

2 At present the saving rate shows a tendency to decrease, depreciation on recently acquired equipment increases and production costs tend to increase. Until recently the production cost per unit in the key companies went down, because—due to low wages— the productivity increase more than compensated for the increase in capital costs. Result: an increase in productivity—as value of production per work hour—can be the only solution.

3 Private short-term debt to foreign countries represents a serious problem: since 1957, this net private debt has increased by $1.6 billion. The Government has instructed the banks not to give

higher interest on short-term loans. 20% of the liabilities to foreigners had to be kept in foreign currency. Since February 1963, as much as 35% of the increase in this debt to foreigners has had to be kept in foreign currency. Foreign reserves at the end of 1963 were $1.8 billion.

4 The scale of public national expenditure is rapidly expanding, (24% in fiscal year 1964 over 1963; public loans and investment increased 23% in the same period), while the sources of treasury revenue are being exhausted. These two trends—which contradict each other—have forced the Government to issue bonds (another contradiction?).

B *Labor mobility and productivity*

The main structural defect is that immobility of labor makes a re-allocation of resources impossible and, consequently, the increase in productivity is severely handicapped. It is emphatically repeated that the Japanese enterprise is conscious of its social role and therefore must keep its commitment of hiring graduates every year, on a lifelong basis. Very probably the intrinsic power of economics will force the social structures to change.

C *Market distribution*

It is practically impossible to find anywhere in the world a similarly irrational and anti-economic framework of superimposed channels of distribution. A kind of iron set-up prevents proper integration of the different markets, falsifies prices and wastes resources.

Conclusion

1 Any serious improvement of Japan's economy must tackle the problem of structures.

2 Mere anti-cyclical measures will not be sufficient to cope with conjunctural problems, because they are affected by anti-economic structures.

Small Business in Japan

by Robert K. Paus

Introduction

The concluding remarks of the preceding article spoke of the problems of the economic structures. Here the problem is taken up in more detail and in particular the problem of dual-structure within the Japanese economy.

The Japanese economy is often described as being schizophrenic: in some aspects it is extremely developed, yet in others is still surprisingly underdeveloped. One of the main stigmas of Japanese economic development has been the plight of the small and medium enterprises. Their mortality rate is astoundingly high, and there is little security for them, or for their employees. They are almost completely excluded from the industrial club of big-businessmen, financiers and government officials. In fact small-and-medium sized enterprises are part of a totally different reality of the Japanese economy.

The author begins by defining the legal bounds of small business and then evaluates its place within the Japanese economy as a whole. Once the legal limits and economic limits of the small-and-medium sized enterprises are taken into account, the problem is viewed as the problem of dual-structure.

The reality of this economic phenomenon perceived, the author analyzes the relationship between small business and government. Indubitably it will be the government's responsibility to find a remedy to this diseased sector of the economy. The steps that are taken, will be taken, and should be taken to achieve this goal are the final consideration of the article.

SMALL BUSINESS IN JAPAN

Legal Definition of Small Business—Place of Medium and Small Manufacturing Enterprises in Japan's Industrial Structure (Establishments, Persons Employed)—Dual Structure—Subcontracting—Competition—Government and Small Business (From Meiji Restoration to the End of World War I, Between the Two World Wars, During World War II, Post-World War II, The "Doubling National Income Plan" (1961–70), Medium Term Economic Plan (1964–68), Government Organizations for Small Business Financing)—Notes—Tables.

The Japanese term for Small Business is *Chūshōkigyō* (Medium and Small Enterprise.) This contracted term in itself probably indicates that we have to do with a particular socio-economic institution, and that Small Business in Japan is not only a question of size. Whether *Chūshōkigyō* is a characteristic Japanese institution, as some scholars would have us believe, is another question.

During the post-World War II period *Chūshōkigyō* was defined legally in various ways according to the specific objectives of individual laws pertaining to Small Business. The common description of *Chūshōkigyō* in these legal definitions is: a company or individual employing not more than 300 persons (however, when the principal business is commerce or service, then less than 30 persons, and in the case of mining, not more than 1,000 persons).[1] When a definite law stipulates capitalization as the line of demarcation between Small and Big Business in Japan then the limit is put at ¥10 million.

However, whether one takes as criterion the number of employees, or the amount of capital or of sales, it is more important to be aware that we have to do with a statistical universe which covers very dissimilar entities. The ECAFE classification gives the following subdivisions:

cottage industry for home use,

cottage industry for the local market,

small-scale hand industry for the domestic mass market,

handicraft industry for luxury markets at home and abroad,

small-scale hand industry for mass markets abroad, and

small-scale powered industry.[2]

Japanese scholars, too, have come up with different categories in order to elucidate the varied aspects of what they call the Small Business phenomenon.

A recent proposal by Nobuo Noda reflects rather well the difficulties involved in delineating any meaningful classes:

1 "those enterprises which still remain small or medium-sized in spite of their nature and potentials. They can grow into large enterprises, but they remain small or medium-sized for these reasons: (i) they are relatively young; (ii) their markets are limited; (iii) they cannot raise funds or recruit managers except from among their family relations."

2 "those enterprises which are engaged in production or service more suitable for small and medium-sized enterprises than for large ones. . . ."

3 "village blacksmiths, barber shops and general stores which satisfy the immediate needs of people living in the neighborhood."

4 "so-called subcontractors. . . "[3]

The trouble with most of these classifications remains that they are constructed in order to prove a definite theory so that the whole endeavor depends on how close the analysis comes to actual business reality. Preference, therefore, should perhaps be given to a "functional" definition of Small Business, if we want to discuss some aspects of Small Business with special reference to the Japanese situation. Functionally, small enterprises in the manufacturing sector would be characterized by the following:

a) Functional specialization of management is marginal or completely lacking. The small enterprise is essentially a one-man concern,[4] perhaps with but a few assistants.

b) Rather close personal relations of the manager with his assistants and employees.

c) Access to the capital market is missing or poses serious difficulties.

d) The enterprise does not have a dominant position in a major product market.

TABLE I–I PERCENTAGE DISTRIBUTION OF ESTABLISHMENTS
IN MAJOR INDUSTRY GROUPS—1951–63

Year	Total	Mining	Construction	Manufacturing	Wholesale, Retail	Finance, Insurance, Real Estate	Transportation, Communication, Electricity, Gas, Water	Services
1951	100.00	0.42	6.42	15.43	44.81	1.99	3.14	27.97
1954	100.01	1.25	5.64	15.96	48.63	2.23	2.37	24.93
1957	100.00	0.29	5.03	15.30	50.74	2.10	2.75	23.79
1960	100.01	0.27	5.44	15.08	50.42	2.50	2.74	23.56
1963	100.00	0.26	6.11	15.44	48.89	3.42	2.81	23.07

Source: Office of the Prime Minister, Bureau of Statistics. *1963 Establishment Census of Japan.* Vol. VI, p. 23.

TABLE I–2 PERCENTAGE DISTRIBUTION OF PERSONS ENGAGED
IN MAJOR INDUSTRY GROUPS—1951–63

Year	Total	Mining	Construction	Manufacturing	Wholesale, Retail	Finance, Insurance, Real Estate	Transportation, Communication, Electricity, Gas, Water	Services
1951	99.99	3.33	6.63	31.95	23.67	4.85	10.32	19.24
1954	100.01	2.54	6.63	32.98	26.42	3.88	9.78	17.78
1957	99.99	2.41	6.57	34.02	27.16	3.15	9.35	17.33
1960	100.00	1.89	7.46	34.78	26.44	3.44	9.28	16.63
1963	99.99	1.23	8.07	34.83	26.62	3.82	9.08	16.34

Source: Office of the Prime Minister, Bureau of Statistics. *1963 Establishment Census of Japan.* Vol. VI, p. 23.

E

TABLE 2   PERCENTAGE DISTRIBUTION OF PERSONS ENGAGED IN PRIVATE MANUFACTURING ESTABLISHMENTS CLASSIFIED BY SIZE (TOTAL WORKERS), JAPAN, 1960 AND 1963

	Total %		1–3 %		4–9 %		10–19 %		20–29 %		30–49 %	
	1960	1963	1960	1963	1960	1963	1960	1963	1960	1963	1960	1963
Regular Workers	81.46	84.17	17.28	16.10	59.34	60.45	78.92	80.45	85.85	87.00	88.65	90.04
Family Workers	4.15	3.88	33.49	34.71	16.38	15.98	3.54	3.19	0.92	0.78	0.30	0.24
Temporary/Daily Workers	6.19	4.11	1.66	1.21	5.14	4.17	5.71	4.48	4.75	3.81	4.85	3.54
Subtotal	91.80	92.16	52.43	52.02	80.86	80.60	88.17	88.12	91.52	91.59	93.80	93.82
Directors	3.90	3.88	1.40	1.47	6.46	7.26	9.13	9.41	7.70	7.73	5.92	5.95
Individual Proprietors	4.30	3.98	46.18	46.51	12.68	12.14	2.70	2.47	0.78	0.67	0.28	0.23
Total	100.00	100.02	100.01	100.00	100.00	100.00	100.00	100.00	100.00	99.99	100.00	100.00

	50–99 %		100–199 %		200–299 %		300–499 %		500–999 %		1,000 or more %	
	1960	1963	1960	1963	1960	1963	1960	1963	1960	1963	1960	1963
Regular Workers	90.11	92.00	90.90	92.96	91.36	93.99	91.00	94.31	91.09	95.03	91.19	95.15
Family Workers	0.08	0.05	0.01	0.01	0.01	0.00	0.00	0.00	0.00	0.00	0.00	0.00
Temporary/Daily Workers	5.59	3.89	6.52	4.51	6.92	4.44	7.79	4.56	8.24	4.35	8.58	4.6
Subtotal	95.78	95.94	97.43	97.48	98.28	98.43	98.79	98.87	99.33	99.38	99.77	99.81
Directors	4.16	4.01	2.55	2.51	1.71	1.56	1.21	1.13	0.66	0.61	0.23	0.19
Individual Proprietors	0.07	0.05	0.01	0.01	0.00	0.00	0.00	0.00	0.00	0.00	0.00	0.00
Total	100.01	100.00	99.99	100.00	99.99	99.99	100.00	100.00	99.99	99.99	100.00	100.00

Source: For 1960-data: Office of the Prime Minister, Bureau of Statistics. *1960 Establishment Census of Japan*, Volume I. Tokyo: OPMBS, January 1962.
For 1963-data: Office of the Prime Minister, Bureau of Statistics. *1963 Establishment Census of Japan*, Volume I. Tokyo: OPMBS, March 1965.

e) The small enterprise remains closely integrated with the local community because of local ownership, management, resources of raw materials or market.

Place of Medium and Small Manufacturing Enterprises in Japan's Industrial Structure.

According to the most recent *Census of Manufactures—1962,*[5] 99.33% of manufacturing establishments are in the Medium and Small Enterprises category, and they employed 67.87% of the persons engaged in

TABLE 3

PERCENTAGE OF ESTABLISHMENTS AND PERSONS ENGAGED CLASSIFIED AS MEDIUM AND SMALL MANUFACTURING ENTERPRISES—1962

		ESTABLISH- MENTS	PERSONS ENGAGED
18	Food and Kindred Products	99.74%	86.59%
20	Textile Mill Products	99.40	73.34
21	Apparel and Other Finished Products	99.86	94.26
22	Lumber and Wood Products	99.94	96.54
23	Furniture and Fixtures	99.91	94.26
24	Pulp, Paper and Paper Worked Products	99.22	73.13
25	Publishing, Printing and Allied Industries	99.38	76.95
26	Chemical and Allied Products	95.82	38.14
27	Petroleum and Coal Products	96.77	57.25
28	Rubber Products	95.37	37.97
29	Leather and Leather Products	99.73	86.26
30	Ceramic, Stone and Clay Products	99.32	75.62
31	Iron and Steel	96.56	37.33
32	Non-Ferrous Metals and Products	96.47	41.96
33	Fabricated Metal Products	99.62	86.64
34	Machinery	98.72	65.16
35	Electrical Machinery, Equipment and Supplies	96.67	42.03
36	Transportation Equipment	97.67	39.71
37	Measuring and Surveying Instruments	98.62	60.15
39	Miscellaneous Manufacturing Industries	99.76	86.19

Source: Ministry of International Trade and Industry (MITI).
   Minister's Secretariat, Research and Statistics Division.
   Census of Manufactures 1962, Report by Industries.
   Tokyo: MITI, December 1964

manufacturing. (Table 1 & 2) Naturally some subdivisions of manufacturing are more and others less concentrated than those averages would indicate. The same holds true when regional divisions by prefecture are considered; some prefectures have more Small Business than others. Industries which have lower percentages for both establishments and persons engaged are: Chemical and Allied Products, Transportation Equipment, Rubber Products, Iron and Steel, Electrical Machinery, Non-Ferrous Metals and Products, Measuring and Surveying Instruments,[6] Machinery, Petroleum and Coal Products. (Table 3)

A *Establishments*

Since 1947 the overall number of establishments has grown at a smaller rate[7] than the number of persons employed. This indicates a tendency towards concentration.

In manufacturing there were 619,703 establishments in 1963 or 15.44% of the Census population. 99.95% of those establishments were privately owned in 1963, and of these 67.58% were listed as individual propri etorships, 32.34% as corporations[8] (Table 4) and 0.08% as unincorporated associations. Among corporations in manufacturing, joint-stock companies accounted for 61.19% in 1963, limited companies for 29.29% and partnerships for 7.15%.

In 1963 major industry groups in manufacturing which accounted for more than 5% of manufacturing establishments were: Food and Kindred Products, Textile Mills, Lumber and Wood Products, Fabricated Metal Products, Apparel and Other Finished Products, and Machinery, in that order. (Table 5)

B *Persons Employed*

Concerning employment one should note that in 1963 65.42% of regular workers employed in manufacturing were engaged in Medium and Small Enterprises. (Table 6) For the class of temporary and daily workers the proportion was 65.95%, and for family workers just a little less than 100% (99.999%). Table 1 (page 64) shows that the percentages for these three types of employees were respectively 84.17%, 4.11% and 3.88% for all manufacturing firms in 1963. Since 1960 the number of

TABLE 4

CORPORATIONS IN MANUFACTURING

PERCENTAGE DISTRIBUTION OF INCORPORATED

ESTABLISHMENTS AND PERSONS ENGAGED

CLASSIFIED BY NUMBER OF TOTAL WORKERS—1963

	NUMBER OF ESTABLISHMENTS	%	NUMBER OF PERSONS ENGAGED	%
Total	200,320	100.00	8,541,507	100.02
1—3	10,330	5.16	25,517	0.30
4—9	54,172	27.04	350,735	4.11
10—19	56,106	28.01	768,929	9.00
20—29	26,334	13.15	626,020	7.33
30—49	23,202	11.58	871,979	10.21
50—99	16,691	8.33	1,135,644	13.30
100—199	7,515	3.75	1,029,462	12.05
200—299	2,353	1.17	568,444	6.66
300—499	1,705	0.85	648,031	7.59
500—999	1,152	0.58	794,319	9.30
1,000 or more	760	0.38	1,722,427	20.17

Source: Office of the Prime Minister, Bureau of Statistics.

1963 Establishment Census of Japan. Volume I, All Japan I, p. 357.

Note 1: "Corporation. . .the establishment which is legally incorporated under law, for instance, company, trade union, cooperative and other associations, miscellaneous corporations." *Ibid.*, p. 6.

TABLE 5

PERCENTAGE DISTRIBUTION OF ESTABLISHMENTS
AND PERSONS ENGAGED IN TWO–DIGITS
MANUFACTURING INDUSTRIES—1963

		ESTABLISH- MENTS	PERSONS ENGAGED
Manufacturing		100.01%	99.99%
18	Food and Kindred Products	16.89	10.54
20	Textile Mill Products	16.51	13.69
21	Apparel and Other Finished Products	6.18	3.68
22	Lumber and Wood Products	9.49	5.25
23	Furniture and Fixtures	4.92	2.35
24	Pulp, Paper and Paper Worked Products	3.01	3.22
25	Publishing, Printing and Allied Industries	4.35	4.13
26	Chemical and Allied Products	1.42	5.27
27	Petroleum and Coal Products	0.13	0.41
28	Rubber Products	0.47	1.53
29	Leather and Leather Products	1.66	0.85
30	Ceramic, Stone and Clay Products	4.72	4.89
31	Iron and Steel	1.04	4.64
32	Non-Ferrous Metals and Products	0.64	1.72
33	Fabricated Metal Products	8.52	6.78
34	Machinery	5.72	9.15
35	Electrical Machinery, Equipment and Supplies	2.24	8.32
36	Transportation Equipment	2.22	6.56
37	Measuring and Surveying Instruments	1.24	2.05
39	Miscellaneous Manufacturing	8.64	4.96

Source: Office of the Prime Minister, Bureau of Statistics.
　　　1963 Establishment Census of Japan. Volume VI, pp. 90-99.

regular workers increased, while the percentage of family workers and temporary/daily workers diminished slightly. The amount of this change for the different sizes of establishments can be read from the same table.

In establishments with less than 30 persons, the proportion of regular workers remained less than 90% in 1963. Although the average percentage of family workers, presumably most of them unpaid, was 3.88%, their proportion in the smaller manufacturing enterprises was for the respective firm-size: (1-3 persons) 34.71%, (4-9 persons) 15.98%, and (10-19 persons) 3.19%. For all other classes of establishments the number of family workers employed was less than 1%.

The employment of temporary and daily workers was much more evenly spread between the different size-classes, except for a low proportion (1.21%) in the smallest class (1-3 persons). Temporary and daily workers accounted for between 3.54% and 4.66%, with an average of 4.11% employed in manufacturing. These differences influence seriously the employment structure in Japanese manufacturing enterprises. Some of them lead one to interpret the relations between people engaged in Small Business as patterned on the family. That this type of employment structure had definite repercussions on the wage differences[10] between different sizes of enterprises seems natural. However, one should not

TABLE 6

MEDIUM AND SMALL MANUFACTURING
ESTABLISHMENTS AND PERSONS ENGAGED
AS PERCENTAGE OF ALL ESTABLISHMENTS AND
PERSONS ENGAGED IN MANUFACTURING 1963

	ALL MANU-FACTURING	MEDIUM AND SMALL	(B) AS % OF (A)
Establishments	619,703	616,025	99.41
Persons Engaged	10,462,406	7,254,735	69.34
Individual Proprietors	416,393	416,386	99.998
Family Workers	403,887	403,881	99.999
Directors	406,104	390,377	96.13
Employees	9,236,022	6,044,091	65.44
Regular	8,806,318	5,760,711	65.42
Temporary/Daily	429,704	283,380	65.95

Source: Office of the Prime Minister, Bureau of Statistics.
    1963 Establishment Census of Japan, Volume I, p. 129.

TABLE 7

VALUE ADDED PER WORKER ESTABLISHMENTS

CLASSIFIED BY NUMBER OF TOTAL WORKERS

1960 AND 1962

PERSONS ENGAGED	TEXTILE MILL PRODUCTS VALUE ADDED PER WORKER		FURNITURE AND FIXTURES VALUE ADDED PER WORKER	
	1960	1962	1960	1962
4—9	22.4	29.0	26.5	38.4
10—19	27.2	36.0	29.4	42.4
20—29	32.5	42.4	32.0	47.5
30—49	35.0	45.3	35.8	48.7
50—99	36.3	48.4	36.7	58.5
100—199	38.4	49.1	45.1	64.2
200—299	39.8	51.2	40.4	67.5
300—499	44.7	56.0	41.8	96.2
500—999	53.7	63.4	38.9	(
				(48.7
1,000 or more	60.9	72.0		(

UNIT: ¥1,000

PERSONS ENGAGED	CHEMICAL AND ALLIED PRODUCTS VALUE ADDED PER WORKER		MACHINERY VALUE ADDED PER WORKER	
	1960	1962	1960	1962
4—9	42.5	59.6	32.1	45.4
10—19	59.9	73.8	37.4	52.1
20—29	66.3	86.1	43.0	58.5
30—49	81.1	92.3	47.3	64.1
50—99	92.7	105.7	54.7	72.6
100—199	108.4	136.4	59.8	80.5
200—299	135.7	142.4	81.2	79.1
300—499	125.8	131.0	75.3	91.3
500—999	187.9	173.0	109.8	109.0
1,000 or more	129.5	169.4	61.6	128.0

Source: Compiled from MITI, *Census of Manufactures 1960, Report by Industries,* and
Census of Manufactures 1962, Report by Industries.

necessarily relate lower wages in Small Business to lower productivity. (Table 6)

99.55% of the persons employed in 1963 were at work in privately-owned establishments. The major proportion, 82.01%, worked in corporations and only 17.96% in individual proprietorships. This corroborates the general opinion that smaller enterprises are usually run by individual proprietors. (Table 8)

Among the corporations in manufacturing, the joint-stock companies employed 86.67% of the persons engaged, limited companies 9.61% and partnerships 2.80%. (Table 9) While medium and small manufacturing corporations account for 98.19% of the total number of corporations in manufacturing, they employ only 62.96% of the persons engaged. This has some bearing on the rate of unionization in Japan.

In 1963 major industry groups in manufacturing employing more than 5% of the persons engaged were the following: Textile Mill Products, Food and Kindred Products, Machinery, Electrical Equipment and Supplies, Fabricated Metal Products, Transportation Equipment, Chemical and Allied Products, Lumber and Wood Products, in that order. (Table 5)

TABLE 8

INDIVIDUAL PROPRIETORSHIP IN MANUFACTURING,
PERCENTAGE DISTRIBUTION OF ESTABLISHMENTS,
AND PERSONS ENGAGED CLASSIFIED BY
NUMBER OF TOTAL WORKERS—1963

	NUMBER OF ESTABLISHMENTS	%	NUMBER OF PERSONS ENGAGED	%
Total	418,615	100.01	1,870,060	99.99
1—3	249,433	59.59	508,625	27.20
4—9	132,552	31.66	732,715	39.18
10—19	28,433	6.79	363,657	19.44
20—29	5,141	1.23	119,747	6.40
30—49	2,252	0.54	81,797	4.37
50—99	691	0.17	44,373	2.37
100 or more	113	0.03	19,226	1.03

Source: Office of the Prime Minister, Bureau of Statistics.
1963 Establishment Census of Japan. Volume 1, All Japan 1, p. 271.
Note 1: "Individual Proprietorship. . .the establishment which is not incorporated and managed by an individual on his own account. It includes the establishment under joint management of individuals." *Ibid.*, p. 6.

TABLE 9—1

MANUFACTURING ESTABLISHMENTS
AS PERCENTAGE OF ESTABLISHMENTS
IN ALL INDUSTRIES CLASSIFIED BY
TYPE OF ORGANIZATION—1963

	ALL INDUSTRIES (A)	MANU- FACTURING (B)	(B) AS % OF (A)
Total	4,016,474	619,703	15.43%
Private	3,903,149	619,403	15.87
Individual Proprietorships	3,007,219	418,615	13.92
Corporations	879,349	200,320	22.78
Joint-Stock Companies	443,445	122,561	27.64
Limited Companies	209,791	58,675	27.97
Limited or Unlimited Partnerships	48,229	14,329	29.71
Mutual Insurance Companies or Foreign Companies	7,940	15	0.19
Trade Union, Cooperative and Other Associations	60,883	4,361	7.16
Miscellaneous Corporations	109,061	359	0.33
Unincorporated Associations	16,581	468	2.84
Local Government	85,300	180	0.21
Government	19,237	44	0.23
Public Corporations	8,788	76	0.86

Source: Office of the Prime Minister, Bureau of Statistics.
   1963 Establishment Census of Japan. Vol. 1, All Japan I, pp. 10 and 25.

TABLE 9—2

PERSONS ENGAGED IN MANUFACTURING
AS PERCENTAGE OF PERSONS ENGAGED
IN ALL INDUSTRIES CLASSIFIED BY
TYPE OF ORGANIZATION—1963

	ALL INDUSTRIES (A)	MANU- FACTURING (B)	(B) AS % OF (A)
Total	30,145,236	10,462,406	34.71%
Private	27,346,517	10,415,178	38.09
Individual Proprietorships	8,582,908	1,870,060	21.79
Corporations	18,701,732	8,541,507	45.67
Joint-Stock Companies	14,519,302	7,403,182	50.99
Limited Companies	2,000,858	820,646	41.01
Limited or Unlimited Partnerships	548,427	239,074	43.59
Mutual Insurance Companies or Foreign Companies	287,264	734	0.26
Trade Union, Cooperative and Other Associations	593,202	69,606	11.73
Miscellaneous Corporations	752,679	8,265	1.10
Unincorporated Associations	61,877	3,611	5.84
Local Government	1,496,846	4,310	0.29
Government	554,237	11,177	2.02
Public Corporations	747,636	31,741	4.25

Source: Office of the Prime Minister, Bureau of Statistics.
1963 Establishment Census of Japan. Vol. 1, All Japan I, pp. 10 and 25.

Dual Structure (Nijūkōzō)

The organizational structure of the Japanese economy has been called, since the publication of the 1956–57 *Economic Survey of Japan,* the 'dual structure' of the Japanese economy. This White Paper identifies the dualism primarily as a structural polarization of labor in large enterprises (over 1,000 employees) and small firms (under 100 persons engaged) with concomitant prevalence of family labor, wage differentials, special relations between small business and the agricultural population, and duality in the structure of exports. However, the fundamental nature of that lopsided structure is indicated much clearer as follows: " . . .two kinds of societies—one of more advanced nature and the other of less advanced stage—exist side by side in Japan. It is for this reason that Japan is called the 'semi-advanced' country among the countries of the world."[12]

Although it might seem superfluous to draw the reader's attention to the distinction made between the dualistic nature of the economy in emerging nations and the dual structure of the present Japanese economy it would help to evaluate the role of *chūshōkigyō.* By dualism is usually understood a specific feature of the early industrialization process, namely ". . .the prolonged coexistence and cohabitation of modern industry and of preindustrial, sometimes neolithic, techniques. This 'dualistic' character of developing countries is to be noted not only with respect to methods of production and distribution; it exists also in attitudes and in ways of living and doing business."[13] Dualism stresses, therefore, more the distance between those two main sectors of an industrializing economy. When Japanese scholars and businessmen speak about the 'dual structure' of Japan's economy they probably focus more on the mutual relations, on the complementarity of large and small business in Japan. As economic history and statistical research have shown, Japan left the stage of *dualism* before World War I, and the national economy has since then been better characterized by what in the last eight years it has become the fashion to call '*dual structure.*'

How does this complementarity now operate organically? In general it can be described in terms of relative scarcity of capital and relative abundance of labor. Whatever you may read about a shortage of labor, which usually means 'skilled' labor, Japan still has a surplus in the form of underemployment.

"From an *international* viewpoint, although capital intensity in large enterprises is said to be high, the level is still lower (in Japan) than in developed countries. Therefore, these enterprises use a system whereby they complement a productivity relatively lower than the international level by low wages in subcontracting medium and small enterprises. From a *national* viewpoint, the scarcity of capital brings about capital concentration in large enterprises in order to use more efficiently a scarce resource, and at the same time, it brings about the dependence of medium and small enterprises on labor-intensive methods of production, as well as an incentive to be subordinated to large-scale enterprises as subcontractors in order to escape the instability of management resulting from poor and outmoded methods of production."[14]

Subcontracting (Shitauke)

In all industrial nations with a modern large enterprise sector the subcontracting system of operations accounts for a predominant proportion of all the work done in small enterprises. Certain parts are manufactured, or some operational steps (e.g. finishing) are carried out by small firms for a larger 'parent' firm *(oyagaisha)* which produces other parts, assembles them and sells the product. This kind of subcontracting is especially prevalent in Japan: examples include the production of special types of paper, paper lanterns and paper umbrellas, doll manufacturing, specialized weaving, fountain pens, cutlery, rubber, rubber articles, and engineering products. The use of the term 'parent' company does not imply necessarily that this firm has any permanent control over the subcontractor, although this might be the impression one gets in Japan. Some 'parent' companies can exercise rather strong control even with 20% of the subcontractor's shares, while other 'parent' firms with a higher part of the equity will have their child *(kogaisha)* much less in hand.

It is clear that the subcontractor is not always a small company, nor does the parent have to be a large enterprise. Small firms may subcontract to other small companies or even to large firms. In many cases, however, the special advantages which a subcontractor may possess are available in small business because of its flexibility or because of its ability to cut overheads.

It might be worthwhile to indicate a few reasons which induce companies to parcel out a part of their operations to smaller firms.

First

A large firm may be operating at what is, for all practical purposes, 100% capacity, and still be unable to meet the deadline for all orders received. This could happen either because it is simply impossible with the actual mechanical capacity, or with the present work force, or because it would increase expenses unexpectedly (for example in cases where overtime rates represent an extremely high premium). This situation could be called the 'capacity' ground for subcontracting.

In Japan the prevalence of subcontracting operates under the 'capacity' ground because parent firms like to reduce the risk of future business fluctuations in demand by partially transferring this imponderable to their subcontractors. It seems to be the rather inflexible human organizational set-up of large companies in Japan which make them especially weak in foreseeing and adapting to market changes. Because Japan depends so heavily on export markets, which by their very nature are less stable than domestic markets, the 'capacity' ground operates very strongly in this country.

Second

Some specific operational step may demand the use of specialized equipment or skill which is not commonly available at moderate expenditures in the regional environment of the parent company, or for which there does not exist a continuous use in the parent firm, even if it could be acquired or hired.

This 'specialization' ground for subcontracting is only another term for differentiation in the industrial organization. Usually it occurs when some specific operation can be done at reduced expenses, if undertaken on a larger scale than would be necessary for the normal production level of a particular parent company. In such a case one subcontractor can perform these operations for different parent companies. (Some auto parts in Japan; Fuji Denki produces practically all motors for tape-recorder manufacturers.) Due to the rapid expansion of industry after World War II, it may be that, while there exist overpopulation and underemployment in rural regions, a shortage of skilled labor arises in urban centers. This seems to be a complementary reason for the wide spread of subcontracting in Japan.

Third

In other cases the subcontractor may possess particular advantages which make it possible for him to provide specific operations at lower cost than the parent company. This situation refers to what one might call the 'special advantage' ground for subcontracting.

In the line of 'special advantages' one might mention the "prevalence of marginal gains in favor of the small entrepreneur in rural areas arising from lower wages and longer working hours, as compared with the higher wages and shorter working hours in the urban large-scale industries."[15] The 'special advantage' of wage differentials is certainly an additional factor accounting for the prevalence of subcontracting in Japan.

Subcontracting is, therefore, not a necessary evil in Japan's economic structure, nor, in terms of organizational theory competition, is it an institution with a heavy dysfunctional character. Perhaps we should underline the advantages accruing to the small subcontractor. The small entrepreneur operating as subcontractor receives a regular flow of raw materials (very important in Japan where the raw material market is dominated by big business and large suppliers), and he is assured of a fairly stable outlet for his product; furthermore he obtains assistance, guidance and financial aid. Technical aid is more prevalent in Japan in the case of one large company and one subcontractor. Financing assistance usually occurs in the case of one parent firm and several subcontractors for the same part. Other aspects of the subcontracting relationship sometimes include strict inspection and quality control by the parent company, and technical advice and loans for equipment. While small firms have been heavy buyers of second-hand machinery, quite a number of subcontractors were obliged to procure very modern pieces of machinery in order to meet the specifications of their parent firms. Financial aid can also take the form of the large company acting as guarantee for securing loans.

Competition (Kyōsō)

To the Western way of thinking the concept of competition is strongly rooted in the ideal of individual achievement. Competition is viewed as the driving force which will reward the producer or seller who provides the best satisfaction for the particular needs of the customer. Competition acts as the motor which makes the market tick as a free market.

Since Japanese psychological attitudes put such a heavy stress on the group, competition has to be delicately controlled inside the group, and most of the time it will take the form of group competition. Once a firm has been accepted into the group (the industry or the subdivision of an industry), the feeling prevails that the group should respect the rules of the game which put a high premium on 'in the field there is place for everyone who belongs.' Naturally this 'place' might very quickly result in a mere subsistence situation for all group members. Competitiveness in the western sense is played down and a higher value is accorded to group cohesion. This explains partially the acceptance of Small Enterprise Cooperative Associations.

This idea about competition squares very well with what the small businessman all over the world means by "a parceling out or a rationing out of the main chance." When Japanese speak or write about competition it seems that they normally imply excessive, cutthroat, or unfair competition.[16] The relative character of the concept appears clearly in such a context. What, then, is specifically meant by excessive competition? a) Competition becomes excessive when it disturbs the balance of trade; b) competition becomes excessive when it gives rise to excess capacity. This again requires the definition of excess capacity.

Profits are revenue minus cost. But both revenue and cost have many other dimensions than the rough price of production and sales, so that competition moves very quickly to the plane of quality competition, packaging competition, competition in distribution channels, and lately more than ever before on the level of substitution (glass, aluminum, stainless steel, concrete, bricks—are all substitutes.)

In the U.S. the anti-trust movement has tried to formulate a concept of fair competition. It usually boils down to a description of unfair competition (which occurs when the public interest is hurt.) However, this public interest seems in most cases to reside in the party or the group of interests which can agitate public opinion in anti-trust proceedings. The fundamental trouble is that there are no hard and clear-cut rules for an economic determination of acceptable competition, and that the legal profession has to work with laws and precedents which are far removed from present day economic reality.

Government and Small Business

A *From the Meiji Restoration to the End of World War I*

The spirit of political renewal which stimulated the young Meiji government also carried over to the economic field. Modernization of industry required a change from cottage industry to factory-type enterprises. Besides the introduction of foreign machinery the organizational setting had also to be adapted, because guilds with their restrictive regulations could not continue to dominate the associations of small entrepreneurial units. The promotion of industry and commerce was pursued under the banner of a bold free trade policy. With the explicit blessing of the government new commercial associations were formed to replace the "feudal" groupings of pre-Restoration time.

A free enterprise system in the field of commercial transactions was outlined in the Commercial Code (Dec. 2, 1880). This early legal document of Japan's modern economic history also encouraged the formation of trade associations on a voluntary basis. However, the first development in manufacturing came after the Ministry of Commerce published the Standing Rules for Trade Association on April 7, 1884. According to these regulations not only farmers but also manufacturers and merchants in the same industry were allowed to form regional associations if two-thirds of the respective enterprises in any area agreed on pursuing common policies. Most of the 300 associations established during the two years' period of 1885–86 exercised a sort of quality control on the products of their members. Old restrictive practices, very similar to those of the pre-Restoration guilds, found their way into the constitutions, and many associations restricted production or fixed prices.

While Small Business clung to old habits and the government was primarily interested in creating large enterprises in the strategic sectors, exports rose sharply after the war with China (1894–95). An alarming flow of poor quality products called for stronger control. Through the enactment of the Key Exports Goods Trade Association Law (1897), the main export producers were forced to become members. Three years later, however, control was extended even to the domestic market through the inclusion of all major manufacturing goods. The number of these trade associations rose from 148 in 1901 to 1,473 in 1924. Control did not only mean quality inspection but also production quotas and agreements fixing price, commission, brokerage fee and even wages.

Although the grouping of Small Business during the first decades of the Meiji Era might be interpreted as a carry-over from former times rather than a defense against infant large enterprises, the pressure of big business competition became serious from the turn of the century on. In 1900 the Industrial Association Law was passed. It provided for the formation of manufacturers, cooperatives with the main goal of joint action in the purchase of raw materials, in production and marketing. In the agricultural sector these associations were rather successful. However, the strong grip of wholesalers on small size manufacturers prevented the effectiveness of the few cooperatives which were launched in the secondary and tertiary sector. To summarize, during the transition period from agricultural to industrial society in Japan (Meiji Restoration to World War I) the major weaknesses of small enterprises had already come to light: a need for cooperative efforts to control quality, to purchase raw materials and to regulate price fluctuations, furthermore a defense against the inroads of big business and the pressure of wholesalers.

B *Between the Two World Wars.*

As long as large enterprises were entangled in their own growth processes, life was still bearable, but the unique opportunities for export expansion during World War I tempted large enterprises to branch out into foreign trade while monopolizing whole sections of the domestic markets, too. From this period on the problems of Small Business were structural. It would take the depression of the early 1920's, though, and the destruction of the large industrial Tokyo-Yokohama area in the Great Earthquake of 1923, to bring the lesson home. A growing awarenesss that the new industrial structure of the 1920's rested on a deep-rooted duality cannot easily be dismissed. Whether this consciousness was primarily due to the agitation of intellectuals influenced by Marxist economic and social theories[17] or by the consequences for Japan's economy under renewed international competition remains outside the limits of this discussion. However, in the decade between 1920 and 1930 the "Small Business problem" became a lively topic with political importance, so the government could not evade its implications. Policies of alleviating the serious population pressure and the economic insecurity caused by erratic business cycles during that period remained foremost on the agenda. Was this governmental concern only dictated by external manifestations of the problem as expressed in widespread unemployment, increased domination of smaller enterprises by big business, the financial struggle of smaller business units ending very often in bankruptcy and the "cut-throat" competition inside the Small Business sector of a particular industry?

Most of the young vigor of the early Meiji government had gone, and concern over Small Business which kept the majority of Japan's population alive and at work took the form of ineffective reiteration of former legislation, as in the 1915 Key Export Products Law. History would repeat itself to include all major manufactured products in the 1931 revision, entitled the Industrial Association Law. While the World Depression of 1929 and increased cartelization among large enterprises required stronger defense on the side of Small Business, its only refuge lay in following this trend. The industrial associations were, in fact, control organizations, so that the whole Japanese economy spontaneously prepared for a quasi-planned economy.

c *During World War II*

Through the 1937 revision of the Industrial Association Law this form of associative organization became available to all the manufacturing industries. Furthermore, government control grew more intense, and two years later the main purpose of the industrial association shifted to rationing of resources. The overall significance of industrial associations for Small Business was that this set-up helped the inefficient companies survive while it limited very seriously the more progressive ones. Small enterprises became so indoctrinated with a spirit of dependence on government protection or of close relationship with big business as sub-contractors that these aspects of the industrial structure in Japan are even now widely regarded as pertaining to the nature of mutual inter-dependency.

The progress of World War II saw two further developments. Through the industrial associations, which took more and more the form of sectorial cartels with government blessing, large enterprises managed the whole raw material market. In 1943, however, the last remnants of a free enter-prise system were removed by the Commercial and Industrial Associa-tion Law which abolished these types of associations, and replaced them with equipment associations under the strict direction of the Control Board. While the contribution of large business to war efforts has mostly been treated as a conspiracy, the political and organizational pressure on Small Business did not absolve industry from being completely dedicated to the national cause, even when it meant a complete shift to the produc-tion of military supplies, or the dismantling of facilities considered of no strategic value.

D *Post-World War II*

If Japan had to be rebuilt on a democratic basis, then the legal framework had to abolish the industrial structure of commercial and industrial associations as the first step toward a free enterprise system. The need for post-war regulation of raw material supply took most of the effectiveness out of the Commercial and Industrial Cooperatives Law (January 1946). In fact, however, these cooperatives were only fictitious reorganizations of the control associations during the war. While there was little political pressure on the part of Small Business in general for greater freedom of action, the overall atmosphere of the enterprise system was funda-mentally influenced, at least legally, by the Anti-Monopoly Law (April 14, 1947). While the 1948 Association Law meant further progress of democratic economic policies, Small Business became an immediate object of administrative policy in the Smaller Enterprise Cooperative Law (July 1949), a thorough revision of the former Commercial and Industrial Cooperatives Law.

A further development in 1948 was the creation by law of the Smaller Enterprise Agency (SEA) as an integral part of the Ministry of International Trade and Industry (MITI), and on the same level as the Patent Agency. The objective was to provide governmental aid for a healthy expansion of Small Business while fully recognizing its value in the economic recovery of Japan. For the first time a coordinating organ for all policy measures concerned with Small Business was established. Its main functions can be described as the development and implementation of the basic policies followed by the government in order to meet the specific problems affecting small industry and other small business units. The Agency performs also a consultant's role by collecting, analyzing, and spreading free information under the direction of a staff of technical and management experts. Initially the organization of cooperatives for mutual assistance between small scale enterprises was also entrusted to the SEA. Furthermore, it played an important role in securing financial sources from different government finance corporations. The promotion of goods produced by Small Business also fell under its jurisdiction. The government counted on this bureaucratic set-up, and on the guidance provided by the Anti-Monopoly Law, to strengthen the overall position of smaller enterprises. On the other side a definite policy of stimulating key industries for the rehabilitation of the economic structure, a lot of hesitation to implement the provisions of the anti-trust legislation, and subsequent mitigating amendments gave rise to complaints that the government fostered oppressive competition from big business.

Further action on the part of the Japanese government was from now on going to be dictated by the overall economic problems as they affected small scale enterprises. Structural aspects of the Small Business problem were left to the SEA until the *New Long-Range Economic Plan* (1961–70) gave authoritative attention to the "dual structure."

One of the central problems nagging Small Business became only too apparent with the recurrent downswings of post-war business cycles in Japan. The financial difficulties hampering small enterprises caused serious concern when the Bank of Japan tightened credit in the autumn of 1953, and again during the 1955–56 recession. Vulnerability of the Small Business sector did not only consist of difficulties in obtaining loans, but more specifically an overall shortage of working capital due to delayed payments by large enterprises for subcontracting jobs. Over the years a series of counter-measures on the part of the government endeavored to alleviate this financial pressure. The legal framework which provides institutions geared to aid Small Business with long- and short-term funds is embodied in the following laws: Law Concerning Financial Business by Cooperatives (June 1, 1949), Medium and Small Enterprise Credit Insurance Law (December 14, 1950), Medium and Small Enterprise Finance Corporation Law (August 1, 1953), Credit Guarantee Association Law (August 10, 1953), and Medium and Small Enterprise Credit Insurance Public Corporation Law (April 26, 1958).

A second area of fundamental trouble for quite a number of small enterprises was their failure to follow the rapid post-war growth process. Once the period of economic recovery was completed, business activity was highly activated by the modernization and rationalization[18] programs of big business, especially in their production facilities and methods during the 1951–56 boom. Renovation of traditional marketing would only set in after the 1957–58 recession. Some subcontractors in the rapidly developing industries participated in the process of production modernization, but the majority of small enterprises were not able or did not manage to steer into that current. Pressure for improved technical standards and equipment modernization was the direct aim of the government when it passed the Medium and Small Enterprise Organization Law (November 25, 1957).

By this time, however, the Economic Planning Agency in particular had become fully aware of the necessity of tackling the Small Business problem in Japan as an integral element of economic structure. Although the post-war period witnessed the passage of a laudable series of legislation concerned with Small Business, no real Small Business policy had been adopted. It required first of all an awareness that difficulties affecting Small Business are intimately connected with the structure of the Japanese economy. Secondly, that a particular problem in the Small Business sector, whether of an organizational, a managerial or a financial nature, be viewed not separately but in close and mutual relationship to the others. Finally, the structural viewpoint postulates a new attitude fully aware of the time-element and possible, even necessary, change which this involves.[19] That the time had come for this attitudinal consciousness manifests itself in the fact that long-range planning got serious attention, overall objectives were set together with the gradual steps leading up to them, and the role of Small Business in such an economic growth process was seriously analyzed.

E *The "Doubling National Income Plan" (1961–70)*[20]

In the framework of Part III, Chapter III *Advancement of Industrial Structure and Correction of Dual Structure,* this plan offers some observations and recommendations on the 'Modernization of Small- and Medium-size Enterprises.'[21] The observation, although in rather general terms, that Small Business will not undergo a quick and drastic change in position as subcontractor and as major exporter seems quite realistic. The modernization goal is presented as hinging on an increase of productivity, with, as subgoals in that direction: 1. adjustment of differences between enterprises, differences influenced by an unequal structural (economic?) and social environment, 2. size-optimization,[22] 3. equipment modernization, 4. removal of the stronger effects on Small Business exercised by the business cycle, 5. modernization in labor relations. For most of these subgoals the Government is asked to act as guide and to provide assistance in cooperation with private initiative. The plan is fairly balanced, and remains so even when it lists the "measures to be emphasized." A special field of governmental action and policy is indicated as follows:

"To push promotion measures suitable to each industry, strengthening of guidance on managerial technique and labor control, promotion of industrialization of new technical know-how, rationalization of taxation, strengthening of vocational training and establishment of employment exchange agencies on a wider regional scale, and improvement of economic conditions for those areas where small- and medium-size enterprises cluster."[23]

The Doubling National Income Plan gave the signal for more regional planning in favor of Small Business, especially at the prefectural level, which had been lagging in economic growth. As long as high rates of overall growth were booked it also stimulated the tendency to increase funds for Small Business financing. However, at the least sign of slackening progress the danger exists that Small Business, as an insecure risk, will find greater difficulty in obtaining loans. This situation becomes an even greater burden in view of the high dependency of enterprises in

Japan on debt capitalization, not only for investment, but also for working capital.

It naturally took time to put the government machinery in working order, and in the meantime the quick realization of some of the other targets necessitated a revision of the plan.

F *Medium-Term Economic Plan. (1964–68)*

Japan's economy, because of the very nature of its rapid growth (9.9% in terms of real GNP—1960 prices—from 1953 to 1963[24]) was subject to a serious imbalance.[25] In Chapter VII, *Modernization of Low-productivity Sectors,* particular attention is paid to Small Business.[26]

This section testifies to a growing awareness of the change process and its serious effects on Small Business. The *Medium-Term Economic Plan* suggests immediately that

"it is important for small business correlated with heavy and chemical industries, where economy of scale is predominant, to establish a set-up of mass production in accordance with the type and the status of the enterprise through intensifying investment of capital equipment, and to encourage amalgamation of small enterprises, development of small businesses, which includes the conversion of family-type management into a judicial person on a cooperative basis and specialization in each field of the sector."[27]

For "goods produced by light industry" the Plan underlines the necessity of a positive policy for high quality products and unique design. National and public experimental institutions are supposed to stimulate private initiative in this line. Increase of productivity, as key to Small Business modernization, requires thirdly ameliorated market research, and last but not least the training of managers. On this point the Smaller Enterprise Agency and the Japan Productivity Center have made tremendous efforts. However, as in all countries, the distribution of information remains only partly effective as long as the small businessman himself does not change his attitude.

Furthermore, Government guidance is indicated for correcting the business environment through strict enforcement of the Law for Preventing Payment Delay to Subcontractors. The plan points out very succinctly that "subcontracting arrangements should be rationalized."[28] The need for a change in attitude is thereby immediately extended to big business.

Since 1963 the Smaller Enterprise Agency has published two White Books on Small Business. The 1964 issue gives some pretty clear indications of modernization forecasts in specific industries.

Summarizing, it becomes clear that with the years the Government, although still closely connected with big business, has directed its attention to the Small Business problem. However, just as investment in social capital (the infrastructure) has been slow in Japan, the pressure groups of Small Business too have lagged in obtaining adequate funds and assistance to redress the situation.

TABLE 10

PERCENTAGE DISTRIBUTION OF SMALL BUSINESS FINANCING
JAPAN, DECEMBER 1962 AND 1963

FINANCING INSTITUTION	PERCENTAGE DISTRIBUTION OF SMALL BUSINESS LOANS & DISCOUNTS OUTSTANDING	
	1962	1963
All Banks:	46.04	44.50
City Banks	20.35	18.91
Local Banks	23.31	23.22
Trust Banks	0.38	0.41
Long-Term Credit Bks.	1.08	1.01
Trust Accounts	0.92	0.94
Small Business		
Financing Institutions	53.96	55.50
Private:	22.04	22.35
Mutual Loans/Savings B.	22.04	22.35
Credit (Loans/Savings)		
Associations	18.87	20.21
Credit Corporative Associations	4.06	4.45
Semi-Private:		
Central Bank for Commercial &		
Industrial Cooperatives	3.80	3.74
Governmental:		
Small Business Finance Corporation	2.88	2.69
People's Finance Corporation	2.31	2.06

Source: The Bank of Japan, Statistics Department.
    Economic Statistics of Japan, 1962 and 1963.

From Table 10 one can easily see that Government financial aid to Small Business is a rather small percent of total loans and discounts, in favor of that economic sector.

G *Government Organizations for Small Business Financing*

The People's Finance Corporation

Established under the People's Finance Corporation Law in June 1949, this institution provides government funds to the general public in order to meet difficulties of obtaining loans from the city, local, trust and long-term credit banks as well as from other financing organizations.

Its major sources of funds are the governmental Trust Fund Bureau and the Post Office Life Insurance. The initial capital of ¥4,000,000,000 in 1950 was gradually increased to ¥20,000,000,000 in 1955. The People's Finance Corporation provides principally loans in small amounts both of a direct and indirect type. In December 1962, ordinary loans which amounted to 89.82% of all loans outstanding to this organization were divided into classes A and B. Class A loans stipulate a maximum of ¥200,000 per person for a 36 months term. Class B loans, with a maximum of ¥500,000 per person, have a 60 months term. 7.25% of the total granted up to December 1962 was loans secured by pensions; the remainder was made up of loans secured by War-Bereaved Family and Repatriation Treasury Bonds and by Resuscitation Loans.

The National Financing Council, an advisory committee, aids the Minister of Finance with the establishment of policies regarding the management of the People's Finance Corporation.

The Medium and Small Enterprise Finance Corporation

Article 1 of the Medium and Small Enterprise Finance Corporation Law (Law No. 138, Aug. 1, 1953) states that "the purpose of the Medium and Small Enterprise Finance Corporation is to finance long-term funds necessary for the promotion of business undertaken by medium and small entrepreneurs. . ." The initial capital of ¥11,000,000,000 forthcoming from the Government's General Account was increased to ¥24,160,000,000 in 1955, ¥8,160,000,000 provided for by the Industry Investment Special Account of the Government, and the rest by the General Account. Under the supervision of the Ministry of International

Trade and Industry and the Ministry of Justice, this corporation extends loans to a limited number of industries, under certain conditions. One to five year loans are granted with a maximum of ¥10,000,000 per beneficiary and aimed at modernization of business through increased equipment investment or "more stable" operating capital.

Since its establishment the contribution of funds provided by the Corporation to Small Business has fluctuated around 3% of all loans to Small Business. Since 1954 indirect loans through agencies have been predominant, and in 1962 they amounted to ¥144,766,000,000 or 68.71% of the total assistance from this Corporation. Direct loans occupied 31.15% in the same year. Outstanding loans in 1962 amounted to slightly more than 70% to manufacturing, and in that sector 88.50% of the funds obtained through the Corporation was for equipment.

Semi-Governmental Institution for Small Business Financing:

The Central Bank for Commercial and Industrial Cooperatives

This semi-governmental institution was established under the Central Bank of Commercial and Industrial Cooperatives Law in December 1936. As the oldest financial organization actually functioning, specializing in Small Business financing, its capital is nearly half subscribed by Small Business cooperatives and similar organizations; the rest was contributed by the government.

Only cooperatives and trade associations affiliated with the Bank as well as their members are eligible for loans. In principle the maximum amount is set at ¥100,000,000 to cooperatives and ¥10,000,000 to affiliated firms. In practice these loans are obtained either through one of the 55 branch offices of the Bank located in the prefectural capitals and the major industrial cities or through credit cooperative associations acting as agents for the Bank. In 1962, 3.80% of all loans granted to small business was forthcoming from this institution. 60.10% of these went to the manufacturing sector, and of this contribution 21.33% was destined for equipment funds.

The private sources of its funds are deposits from member organizations and their affiliated firms and a number of financial institutions.

Notes

[1] *Medium and Small Enterprise Finance Corporation Law,* Law #138, Aug. 1, 1953, art. 2, par. 1.

[2] ECAFE, *Economic Survey of Asia and the Far East, 1953* (New York: United Nations, 1953), pp. 9-10.

[3] Nobuo Noda, "Rationalization of Small and Medium-Sized Enterprises," IPCCIOS II/ *Conference Papers*/S-2. 3, pp. 1-2.

[4] While the number of enterprises has been increasing since the end of World War II, the percentage of one-man establishments has steadily diminished. For the years when the Establishment Census was taken the percentage of one-person establishments was respectively 37.14% in 1951, 33.12% in 1954, 29.07% in 1957, 27.90% in 1960, and 27.12% in 1963. Except for this most recent Establishment Census the absolute number of such enterprises has also gone down.

[5] Ministry of International Trade and Industry (MITI), Minister's Secretariat, Research and Statistics Division. *Census of Manufactures 1962, Report by Industries.* Tokyo: MITI, December 1964.

[6] This category includes also: medical instruments, physical and chemical instruments, photographic and optical instruments, watches and clocks.

[7] The respective rates for the Census years were:

Year	Establishments		Persons Engaged	
	Increase %	Yearly % Increase	Increase %	Yearly % Increase
1947	—	—	—	—
1951	12.9	3.1	16.1	3.8
1954	3.0	1.0	8.3	2.7
1957	7.6	2.5	17.2	5.4
1960	3.0	1.0	16.9	5.3
1963	9.4	3.0	16.7	5.3

Cf., Office of the Prime Minister, Bureau of Statistics *1963 Establishment Census of Japan.* Volume VI, Summary, p. 16.

[8] Corporations accounted for the highest proportion in manufacturing, and their number has been increasing while individual proprietorships diminished.

[9] Regular workers are defined in government statistics as: "Regular employees: paid employees who are regularly employed without the specified period of employment." Or "Regular employees: regularly engaged in an establishment." Similarly "Temporary employees: paid employees who are employed for a specific period of more than a month but less than a year", or "Temporary employees: employed for a specific period of more than a month but less than a year." Also "Day laborers: paid employees who are employed daily or for a specific period of less than a month," or "daily employees: employed daily or for a specific period of less than a month." And finally "Unpaid family workers: those who work without wages or salaries in an unincorporated enterprise operated by a member of family," or "unpaid family workers:

the unpaid family member of the self-employed, and working in the business." The first of these dual definitions was adopted by the 1962 *Employment Status Survey*, the second is to be found in the *Year Book of Labor Statistics 1962*.

[10] Cf. Makoto Sakurabayashi, "Interfirm Wage Differentials in Present-Day Japan–Theoretical Framework," Tokyo: Sophia University Socio-Economic Institute Bulletin No. 10, 1966.

[11] Table 7 shows that even in the small selection of minor industry groups presented some classes of Small Business are able to achieve a higher added value per worker than large enterprises in their group.

[12] Economic Planning Agency, *Economic Survey of Japan, 1956–57*, p. 24.

[13] Albert O. Hirschman, *The Strategy of Economic Development* (New Haven and London: Yale University Press, 1958), pp. 125-126.

[14] Kenichi Miyazaki, "The Dual Structure of the Japanese Economy and Its Growth Pattern," *The Developing Economies*, Vol. II, No. 2, (June, 1964), 170.

[15] U.N. Economic Commission for Asia and the Far East, *Report of the Study Group of Small-Scale Industry Experts on Their Visit to Japan*, Document E/CN. 11/I and T/108, 1 Feb. 1955 (Mimeo), p. 22.

[16] Cf., Martin Bronfenbrenner, " 'Excessive Competition' in Japanese Business," *Monumenta Nipponica*, Vol. XXI, Nos. 1-2 114-124.

[17] Reference should here be made to the pre-war discussions between the *Kōza-ha* and the *Rōnō-ha*.

[18] Rationalization acquired, since the inter-war period, a twofold meaning in Japan: 1. a more efficient use of men, materials and equipment in a specific enterprise; 2. an improvement of structural relations in a particular industry, usually an "understanding" between firms to "adjust voluntarily" their production to the depressions of a specific market.

[19] Cf., the *Assumptions* listed as introduction.

[20] Official English title: *New Long-Range Economic Plan of Japan (1961–70)— Doubling National Income Plan*.

[21] Economic Planning Agency. *New Long-Range Economic Plan of Japan (1961– 70)—Doubling National Income Plan*. (Tokyo: The Japan Times, Ltd., 1961), pp. 98-100.

[22] On this point the text of the Plan could not be more realistic when reference is made to the foreseeable result: mergers of marginal enterprises do not guarantee rational economic efficiency.

[23] *Ibid.*, p. 100.

[24] Fiscal years.

[25] Cf., "Problems Accompanied by the Rapid Growth of Economy," in: Economic Planning Agency. *Medium-Term Economic Plan. 1964–68.* (Tokyo: Government Printing Bureau, 1965), pp. 5-8.

[26] *Ibid.*, pp. 59-63.

[27] *Ibid.*, p. 61.

[28] *Ibid.*, p. 62.

CHAPTER V

Japan's Capital Market: Size and Problems

by Yoshio Terasawa

This article deals with the capital market. First, the author gives us the structure of the capital market as a whole. He then studies the market in more detail and points out certain specific problems and possible reforms. Mr. Terasawa briefly compares the capital markets of Japan with those of other developed countries.

Possibly the most outstanding characteristic has been the predominant position of Japanese banks, and their power, in every aspect of financing. Since World War II, Japanese corporations have shown a definite preference for bank borrowings over other methods of financing; this is due primarily to the underdeveloped condition of the Japanese securities market.

The latter cannot properly develop until certain essential reforms are carried through, but also Japanese corporations must place more trust in the securities market, and gradually move away from excessive reliance on the banks. This situation is almost a vicious circle.

Before reforms are to be enacted, there must be full cognizance of the basic problems of the present market system. The author lists four, analyzes them, and proposes the necessary reforms.

JAPAN'S CAPITAL MARKET: SIZE & PROBLEMS

Size of the Capital Market—Predominant Position of the Banks —Basic Problems of the Present Market (Absence of Capital Increase, Stock Investment Trusts as a Factor Exaggerating Market Price Fluctuations, Stock Market Supporting Organizations)—Tables—Charts.

In Japan, only stock exchanges constitute an active capital market in the genuine sense of the expression. Although various kinds of securities, such as Government bonds, municipal bonds, corporate bonds, Government guaranteed bonds and bank debentures are issued, most of them are purchased by financial institutions immediately following issuance, and they rarely circulate among investors. In other words, there is only an issuing market for bonds, but no active trading market for outstanding bonds. (Table 1)

Let us take a look at the size of the Japanese capital markets, which are characterized by a paralysis of bond trading, from two points of view—net yearly increases of securities, and outstanding amounts.

In recent years, total securities have been increasing by approximately ¥1,500 billion per year. (Amount of new issues before deducting amount retired are far bigger than ¥1,500 billion. In 1965 new issues amounted to approximately ¥2,870 billion.) Looking at the breakdown of the increases, securities such as stocks, corporate bonds and bank debentures issued by private enterprises occupied the predominant portion, reaching 70%. The shares of Government guaranteed and municipal bonds, however, have been gaining recently. Of the securities issued by private corporations, stocks are the most popular, but the rate of increase in bank debentures is the highest. Strictly speaking, bank debentures are a little different from other corporate securities, because they are issued by long-term credit banks or by special financial institutions related in one way or another to the Government. Funds raised through the issuance of bank de-

G

TABLE I   NET YEARLY INCREASES OF SECURITIES

(in billions of yen)

	Gov. Bonds Stock Gov. Bills	Municipal Bonds	Special Bonds (1)	Sub-total	Bank Debenture	Corporate Bonds	Stock (2)	Sub-total	Total
1955	90.1	22.1	23.8	45.9	58.6	27.2	110.5	196.3	242.2
1956	(-) 66.2	41.9	37.7	79.7	48.3	58.4	227.0	333.7	413.3
1957	(-) 44.0	25.8	34.5	60.3	73.5	52.5	293.7	419.7	480.0
1958	104.9	18.3	58.4	76.7	148.4	57.6	246.3	452.3	529.0
1959	165.4	20.6	62.7	83.3	191.7	145.9	287.5	625.1	708.4
1960	80.7	37.4	122.0	159.4	230.6	152.1	521.8	904.5	1,063.9
1961	(-) 126.6	26.7	176.6	203.3	210.6	385.7	995.8	1,592.1	1,795.4
1962	55.1	31.5	225.4	256.9	268.8	133.1	793.2	1,195.1	1,452.0
1963	(-) 115.5	65.7	305.4	371.1	373.2	163.9	676.1	1,213.2	1,584.3
1964	114.7	90.5	341.4	431.9	410.5	152.8	867.6	1,430.9	1,862.8
1965	31.5	154.2	604.0	758.2	566.1	219.4	270.0	1,055.5	1,813.7
65/55 (times)		6.9	25.4	16.5	9.7	8.1	2.4	5.4	7.5
Percentage Distribution (%)									
1955		9.1	9.8	18.9	24.2	11.2	45.6	81.0	100.0
1960		3.5	11.5	15.0	21.7	14.3	49.0	85.0	100.0
1961		1.5	9.8	11.3	11.7	21.5	55.6	88.8	100.0
1962		2.2	15.5	17.7	18.4	9.2	54.6	82.2	100.0
1963		4.1	19.2	23.3	23.4	10.3	43.0	81.0	100.0
1964		4.9	18.3	23.1	22.0	8.2	46.6	76.7	100.0
1965		8.5	33.3	41.8	31.2	12.1	14.9	58.2	100.0

Notes: 1.   Government guaranteed bonds issued by public corporations.
       2.   Paid up capital of listed companies.

Source: T. Nakamura, *Kōdō-Seichō to Kinyū*, Tokyo Shōken.

TABLE 2   SOURCES AND USES OF CORPORATE FUNDS

	U.S.A. 1965	Japan Oct. '65 Nov. '66
Sources, Total	100.0%	100.0%
Internal Sources, Total	62.3	39.8
Retained Earnings	22.9	3.0
Depreciation	39.4	36.7
External Sources, Total	37.7	60.3
Stocks	0.4	5.7
Bonds	10.0	9.4
Bank Loans	12.5	35.7
Trade Payables	7.5	4.1
Tax Liabilities & Other Debts	7.3	5.3
Uses, Total	100.0	100.0
Increase in Physical Assets, Total	71.0	55.1
Plant and Equipment	62.9	54.0
Inventories	8.1	1.1
Increase in Financial Assets, Total	29.0	45.0
Receivables	17.5	9.9
Cash and Gov. securities	4.5	15.0
Other Assets (Including Investment)	11.0	20.2
Discrepancy (Uses Less Sources)	—	—

Sources: For U.S.: *Survey of Current Business* May 1966.
For Japan: Bank of Japan, *Honjo Keizai Tōkei, 1966* (Economic Statistics 1966)

TABLE 3   PERCENTAGE DISTRIBUTION OF NET INCREASE
OF SECURITIES (BY TYPE OF ISSUE)

	Japan (1965)	U.S.A. (1964)
Government Issues	33.3%	39.0%
Municipal Issues	8.5	24.5
Bonds & Debentures	43.3	30.0
Stocks	14.9	6.5

Sources: For U.S.: SEC, *Statistical Bulletin*
For Japan: Bank of Japan, *Economic Statistics*

bentures are used mainly for long-term loans to industrial companies.

Stock issuance is very popular and important in the field of financing. We must not, however, neglect the important role played by banks in long-term financing. Table 2 points up this fact clearly and we deal with this matter later.

When we compare net increases of various securities in Japan with those in the United States, obvious differences appear in the structure of both capital markets. Roughly speaking, the net increase of securities in the United States was approximately $22 billion in 1964. Of this amount, Government and municipal securities accounted for 63.5%, or $14 billion. The remaining $8 billion was divided into $6 billion for corporate bonds and $1.4 billion for stocks. (Table 3)

In Japan, the securities outstanding amounted to around ¥13,000 billion at the end of 1965. A comparison of the breakdown of securities outstanding in 1965 with those of 1935 gives us the following changes:

1. The amount of municipal bonds steadily increased. Government guaranteed bonds issued by public corporations appeared again for the first time since the war.
2. The relative importance of corporate bonds and bank debentures increased and stock has not yet resumed its pre-war share in spite of the rush of stock issues in recent years. (Tables 5 & 6)

Generally speaking corporate bonds have far less importance than

TABLE 4   COMPARISON OF CAPITAL MARKETS (END OF 1965)

	U.S.A.	Japan
	—$ billion—	
National Income	559.0	66.3
	(100.0)	(100.0)
Bank Deposits	385.2	57.3
	(68.9)	(86.4)
Market Value of Listed	537.5 NYSE	26.1 TOKYO 1st
Stocks	(96.2)	(39.4) & 2nd
Total Amount of Corporate	127.7	4.9
Bonds Outstanding	(25.0)	(7.4)
Total Assets of Investment	35.2	3.1
Trust	(6.3)	(4.7)

Source: *Manual of Securities Statistics 1966,* Tokyo
Nomura Research Institute

TABLE 5 JAPANESE SECURITIES OUTSTANDING

(in billions of yen)

	Gov. Bonds	Short-term Gov. Bills	Municipal Bonds	Special Bonds	Bank Debentures	Corporate Bonds	Stock	Total
1935	9.9	0.5	2.4	—	1.9	2.7	16.4	33.8
1955	535.5	334.1	92.7	65.8	361.5	227.4	595.0	2,170.1
1960	541.5	578.3	194.6	381.1	1,054.0	692.8	1,888.0	5,330.3
1961	520.9	679.6	221.3	557.7	1,264.6	1,078.4	2,853.8	7,176.3
1962	492.7	581.2	252.8	783.2	1,533.4	1,211.5	3,515.8	8,370.6
1963	461.8	667.2	318.5	1,088.6	1,906.6	1,375.1	4,032.0	9,849.8
1964	440.4	551.6	409.1	1,429.9	2,317.0	1,529.2	4,599.5	11,276.7
1965	408.8	655.5	563.3	2,034.0	2,883.1	1,748.6	4,707.7	13,001.0
65/55 (times)		2.0	6.1	30.9	8.0	7.7	7.9	6.0
Percentage Distribution								
1935	29.3	1.5	7.1	—	5.6	8.0	48.5	100.0
1955	24.7	15.4	2.3	3.0	16.7	10.5	27.4	100.0
1963	4.7	6.8	3.2	11.1	19.4	14.0	40.9	100.0
1964	—	4.9	3.6	12.7	20.5	13.6	40.8	100.0
1965	—	5.0	4.3	15.6	22.2	13.4	36.2	100.0

Source: T. Nakamura, *Kōdo-seichō to Kinyū*, Tokyo Shōken.

TABLE 6 CURRENT TERMS OF ISSUE FOR BONDS & DEBENTURES

Bonds & Debentures	Interest Rate	Issue Price (inc. deferred)	Period of Redemption	Ultimate Yields to Subscribers	Effective as from
	(Annual %)	(per ¥100)	Period	(Annual %)	
Government Bonds Long-term	6.5	¥98.60	7 years	6.795	Jan. '67
Short-term	*¥0.0155	99.70	60 days	5.807	June '53
Municipal Bonds	7.3	99.75	7(2) years	7.354	Apr. '61
Gov't-Guaranteed Bonds	7.0	99.75	7(2) years	7.053	Apr. '61
Corporate Bonds A	7.3	99.50	7(2) years	7.408	Apr. '61
A'	7.3	99.00	7(2) years	7.518	May '61
B	7.3	98.75	7(2) years	7.573	Apr. '61
C	7.5	99.00	7(2) years	7.720	May '61
D	7.5	98.50	7(2) years	7.831	Apr. '61
Bank Debentures	7.3	100.0	5(1) years	7.300	Apr. '61
Interest-bearing	6.8	100.0	3(1) years	6.800	July '62
Pre-discounted	*¥0.016	94.14	1 year	6.224	Apr. '61

*Daily per ¥100
Source: Nomura Securities Ltd., Underwriting Department

stocks in the field of corporate finance. This, together with the relatively small amount of Government issues, is characteristic of the Japanese capital market, and cannot be found in the highly developed capital markets of other countries.

A brief comparison of the capital markets of the United States with those of Japan is given in Table 4.

Predominant Position of Japanese Banks in the Capital Market

There are two sources of corporate funds, internal and external. External sources consist of stock and bond issues, borrowings and trade accounts payable. Funds derived from external sources other than stock issues may be called "outside funds." The ratio of outside funds to total funds used in the United States, Great Britain, Germany, and Japan are compared in Chart I. (page 115)

There is a distinct difference between the U.S.A.-Britain group and the Germany-Japan group in the ratios of outside funds. Germany and Japan, whose growth rates outstripped other countries, relied heavily on borrowed money. The capital investments of both countries far exceeded their retained earnings. Japan, however, has a larger portion of borrowings than Germany, amounting to 34% of total sources of funds. Trade accounts payable created from Japan's popular inter-company credits, followed after borrowings, with a share of 22%. When compared with these two sources, bonds and stock are relatively unimportant. It is true to say that Japanese corporations have given preference to bank borrowings over other methods of financing.

As Table 7, indicates, even investments in fixed production equipment were largely financed by borrowings. Because of this manner of financing, interest charges of corporations increased sharply and their earnings position has become impaired in recent years as a result therof. Banks accordingly wield enormous powers in all aspects of financing.

At this point, I should like to refer briefly to the historical background in an attempt to explain why Japanese corporations became indebted so heavily to banks.

1. From the start of the war through 1950, many industrial plants were shattered and inflation was rampant. With their plants in ruins

TABLE 7 CAPITAL INVESTMENTS AND INTERNAL SOURCES OF FUNDS

Year	Japan		U.S.A.		Great Britain		Germany	
	A	B	A	B	A	B	A	B
1957	37.0	52.8	82.1	113.0	92.2	120.2	87.6	104.2
1958	35.0	53.5	105.7	127.6	96.2	113.5	69.6	77.7
1959	44.8	53.8	121.8	153.6	118.6	147.5	79.0	90.3
1960	40.1	58.8	80.5	108.5	102.7	137.2	68.0	91.8
1961	38.4	64.9	99.4	123.1	76.0	66.3	61.1	78.1
1962	40.4	65.7	106.1	116.6	112.4	101.5	64.1	73.7
1963	49.1	64.8	127.4	97.1	—	—	73.7	77.4
1964	51.5	68.0	134.9	102.3	—	—	79.1	90.4

Source: Bank of Japan, *Kokusai Hikaku Tokei* (International Comparison of Economic Securities)
Notes: A= Internal Sources/Capital Investment
 B= Internal Sources & Stock Issued/Capital Investment

after the end of the war and capital wiped out by inflation Japanese industrialists had to look to the Government for funds for reconstruction purposes. The Bank of Japan, through the Emergency Reconstruction Finance Bank, made huge loans to industry. Private investment was paralyzed and sound finance had to give way in the face of the fundamental need to survive.

With the abatement of such direct loans, they were replaced by loans from commercial banks, which in turn availed themselves of the rediscount facilities of the Bank of Japan. The result was a great reliance on commercial banks and a reliance of commercial banks on the Bank of Japan.

2. The occupation reforms disturbed the old financial structure. The separation of ownership from management was ordered and many active managers were purged. Accordingly, new managers had little understanding of the traditional sources of equity funds. Unfortunately, even after the capital market started to provide facilities for long-term capital, managers more or less neglected the establishment of a sound long-range financing policy in the midst of their frantic attempt to gain market shares for their products. The growing tendency for bankers to move into industrial establishments as managers in charge of finance promoted further preference for bank loans over other financing methods.

3. The dissolution of the *zaibatsu* has had a telling effect. Until the end of the war, the capital requirements of large corporations were met almost entirely by means of the issuance of shares to affiliated corporations under the *zaibatsu* combines or to *zaibatsu* holding companies. With the removal of these sources, equity funds dried up.

4. The traditional practice of rights offering did not help in improving the debt-equity ratio. Rights offerings of new stock at par value to stockholders regardless of the current market price is an ingrained custom which persists to the present day in Japanese stock issues. Such rights offerings have a decided disadvantage from the point of view of the cost of capital.

5. As stated earlier, both Germany and Japan were characterized by a war-devastated economy, a high rate of economic growth since the war and a high ratio of outside funds to total sources of funds. Germany, however, financed approximately 70% of its

TABLE 8 STOCK OWNED BY FINANCIAL INSTITUTIONS

(in billions of yen; at cost)

At the end of	Banks	Trust a/c at Banks	Life Insurance	Non-life Insurance	Mutual Banks	Credit Associations	Total	Investment Trusts
1959	172.1	7.0	124.3	62.6	7.0	3.4	376.7	509.1
1960	231.0	7.6	152.2	76.3	9.4	4.8	481.3	799.6
1961	329.6	13.2	201.9	98.7	12.4	6.5	662.3	920.0
1962	401.4	16.9	252.7	110.3	15.1	7.9	804.5	999.2
1963	484.4	19.5	311.3	126.2	18.9	9.9	970.2	922.9
1964	576.1	23.0	373.2	146.8	23.0	10.2	1,152.4	674.2
1965	612.2	27.2	437.1	152.1	25.1	17.4	1,271.7	583.1
1966 (end June)	665.9	30.2	519.8	162.6	27.0	21.9	1,427.4	

Source: *Zaikai Kansoku*, Tokyo, Nomura Securities Ltd.

capital investment with retained earnings and depreciation, as against 35 to 40% in the case of Japan. This difference is derived from the different policies that both Governments adopted for rehabilitation of their economies.

Germany had a money reform in 1948 and all private debts were devalued to 1/10. Company assets were fully revalued to the then prevailing market price, and yet there was no tax on the re-valuation profits. Companies, therefore, could depreciate enough. In Japan, on the other hand, companies were forced to repay all loans to banks, and if companies could not repay everything to the banks, the remaining balance of the loans was compensated by allotments of new shares to the banks when capital increases were made. Thus an intimate relationship between bank and in-dustrial companies was established, enhancing the power of banks over industry in general. (Table 8) Revaluation in Japan was not sufficient and a revaluation tax was enacted. Allocations for depreciation, therefore, unlike Germany, were not sufficient.

Of course, the under-developed condition of the Japanese securities market is the fundamental reason for the heavy reliance of industrial companies on bank loans.

Basic Problems of the Present Capital Market

A *Absence of Corporate Bond Market*

In the post-war period, bonds were not accepted by investors because they had previously experienced severe inflation. In addition, with the issuing terms subject to government control, the yield was not sufficiently high to attract the interest of individual investors. At the present time 24 issues are listed on the Tokyo Stock Exchange, but there is practically no bond market in Japan.

Table 9 shows that city banks, long-term credit banks, local banks and other financial institutions constitute the largest purchasers, account-ing for more than 80% of the total issues. Japanese banks have a tendency to purchase bonds, not so much as investments in securities but as a modification of long-term loans to their customers. They therefore

TABLE 9 INVESTORS IN NEW ISSUES OF CORPORATE BONDS

(%)

Year	Amount Offered publicly (¥ bil.)	City Banks & Long-term Credit Banks	Local Banks	Trust Banks & Insurance	Agricultural Associations, etc.	Commercial Coopera-tives, etc.	Mutual Loan Banks	Individuals & Others	Investment Trusts
1959	18.1	37.6	32.6	3.6	9.3	2.5	2.6	13.0	2.8
1960	38.1	20.1	15.0	2.0	3.7	1.3	1.8	10.3	45.8
1961	18.8	35.9	17.3	2.1	3.1	2.1	2.1	4.6	33.7
1962	17.1	53.9	26.0	3.3	4.3	2.9	3.3	6.1	0.2
1963	26.9	50.2	25.1	3.5	3.7	2.7	2.6	12.2	0.0
1964	24.8	50.8	24.1	4.8	3.6	2.7	2.9	11.1	0.0
1965	39.1	38.3	22.9	4.8	8.2	6.0	2.3	17.0	0.5
1966									
Jan.	38.1	35.5	20.6	4.7	10.8	5.5	2.3	20.4	0.2
Feb.	37.6	36.7	23.2	5.2	9.0	4.8	2.1	18.9	0.1
Mar.	41.2	34.6	22.5	5.3	10.4	6.2	1.9	18.5	0.6
Apr.	33.1	35.1	22.5	6.0	8.5	5.3	1.9	19.7	1.0
May	40.4	36.4	20.9	6.2	9.3	4.5	1.9	20.0	0.8
June	40.7	35.3	24.0	6.0	9.7	4.6	1.9	18.3	0.2
July	34.2	36.1	22.9	6.3	9.1	5.1	2.3	18.2	0.0
Aug.	27.5	35.8	20.5	6.4	8.2	5.4	2.6	21.2	—
Sep.	24.8	42.8	16.7	6.2	5.0	5.0	2.1	22.2	—
Oct.	32.8	35.4	22.3	7.2	9.0	4.9	2.2	18.9	0.1
Nov.	41.9	34.9	21.5	7.8	9.7	4.0	2.0	20.1	0.0

Source: *Zeikai Kansoku*, Tokyo, Nomura Securities, Ltd.

prefer to purchase their customers' corporate bonds. In practice, they hold such bonds in registered form until maturity, rarely unloading them for sale. Banks have another important reason for buying bonds. They can give bonds as security for loans from the Central Bank and also offer them for sale when the Central Bank enters into buying operations. Indeed, Japanese banks are able to occupy a most important position as the largest purchasers of bonds, due primarily to such financial advantages.

The other basic reason for the absence of a bond market is the disproportionate rate of interest on short- and long-term loans. The issuing rates of bonds are completely regulated by the Government at between 7.4% and 7.8%. Call money rates, on the other hand, fluctuate freely, reflecting monetary conditions. Reflecting the recent trend of easier monetary conditions, the decline in the call rate was marked in fiscal 1965 and 1966; up until 1964, it exceeded the yield on newly issued bonds. (Chart 11, page 116). It is imperative, however, for outstanding bonds to be quoted in a range which does not deviate largely from the rate of new issues, subject to government control. Under these circumstances the exchanges cannot function effectively as a trading market for outstanding bonds.

Since yields of new issues are pegged at far below the prevailing market rates the number of issuers and the amounts of each issue are also regulated by a bond issuing group consisting of banks and securities companies. In order to enable Japanese companies to raise funds more freely through bond issues, it is imperative that there be more flexible issuing terms for bonds. A bond market can only be created by the participation of individual investors who are attracted by bond yields.

Thanks to the recent easier monetary trend, securities companies are suceeding in selling more bonds to the investing public. Bond transactions in the form of cross-transactions are also increasing steadily and as a result, securities companies have started to announce the over-the-counter price of selected bonds once a week, as a first step to the creation of a bond market. On August 1, 1966, The Nippon Express Co. offered to its shareholders convertible debentures in the amount of ¥10,000 million. The initial conversion price was decided in relation to the market price of the common stock. This may be a common practice in Western capital markets, but for Japan it was epoch-making. The conversion price of convertible debentures issued by Japanese corporations in the Japanese capital market, excluding those issued abroad, had always been established in relation to the par value of the common stock. Another new feature on the market was the comparatively large amount of the issue. At any rate, bonds were now made much more attractive. The creation of an active bond market is a basic requisite for the sound development of the domestic capital market.

B *Disadvantages of the Traditional Method of Capital Increase*

On September 16, 1964, The Nippon Miniature Bearing Co. announced a capital increase, with a public offering of 110,000 shares, and with rights offered to shareholders at a ratio of 3 new for 10 old. This announcement was made in spite of the company's policy of no dividend payment for that accounting term. The result was that the stock lost 37 yen in price on the day of the announcement and closed at 50 yen.

Securities companies which handled the company's issue strongly opposed the capital increase and decided not to underwrite the publicly offered shares and the unsubscribed-for shares. This fact is worthy of note because this is the first time that securities companies publicly refused their customers' capital increases.

Unlike some other advanced countries, some Japanese companies use the proceeds of capital increases as working capital, instead of funds for long-term capital investments. This was the case with Nippon Miniature Bearing. There is a growing tendency for companies to resort to capital increases to raise funds when money is not otherwise obtainable. Statistics show that about 46% of the proceeds of rights offerings was used as working funds and for the repayment of bank borrowings in 1964.

Many Japanese industrial companies expanded their production facilities on borrowed money and repaid borrowings later on with the money received from shareholders. Especially at maturity, when money is tight and no further bank credit is available, they are compelled to make rights issues. No matter how poor the general market conditions are, and no matter how uncertain companies' earning prospects are, they can effect rights offerings if the stock is selling above par value.

Until July 1, 1966, shareholders could not sell their subscription rights. In order to recover the ex-rights depreciation in the price of their old shares, they had to subscribe for new shares, even at times when they did not have money at hand. However, under a partial revision of the Japanese Commercial Code, rights to subscribe additional shares became assignable, and warrants can now be traded on the market. Thus, from January 9, 1967 on, warrants of The Nippon Light Metal Co. are traded on a when-issued basis in the Tokyo Stock Exchange. It will help to expedite a more mature development of the Japanese capital market.

In addition, rights offerings do not require any underwriting by securities companies. Accordingly, there is no way that securities companies can screen capital increases in the light of market conditions. The market slump in the past several years is largely related to such an excess of capital increases. (Table 10)

TABLE 10 NEW ISSUES AND DIVIDENDS.

TOTAL FOR ALL THE COMPANIES LISTED ON THE

FIRST MARKET OF THE TOKYO STOCK EXCHANGE

(in millions of yen)

	Shares Issued against Cash Payment (A)	Dividends (B)	(A)—(B)
1958	159,633	122,938	36,695
1959	148,873	138,102	10,771
1960	324,518	174,225	150,293
1961	609,019	230,781	378,238
1962	519,386	307,253	212,133
1963	350,515	345,149	5,366
1964	550,998	391,501	159,497

Source: *Annual Statistics Report,* Tokyo Stock Exchange

The amounts raised during recent years are huge by any standards. The figure for 1961 accounted for 10.8 per cent of the total market price of all the listed shares at the end of the year, far exceeding the aggregate dividends paid out by all the listed companies during the year. Since a substantial part of the capital increases was effected on a rights basis and the aggregate dividends were very much short of the total capital required for subscription, subscribers to the issues—in effect shareholders —were obliged, in addition to the dividends they received, either to find some new source of funds or to dispose of at least a portion of their holdings to pay for the shares allotted.

TABLE 11 RATIO OF DIRECTORS' OWNERSHIP

(9 BIG CORPORATIONS)

	Ratio to Outstanding Shares	Adjusted Ratio 1
1957	0.387%	0.387%
1958	0.415	1.421
1959	0.359	0.366
1960	0.340	0.351
1961	0.315	0.328
1962	0.294	0.309
1963	0.258	0.272
1964	0.243	0.258

Source: *Problems of the Japanese Securities Market,* Tokyo, Nomura Research Institute.
Note 1: Excluding the number of shares sold to persons other than shareholders.

Table 11 shows some interesting figures. Directors of nine big companies (three electric power companies, three steel companies, and three electric appliance producers), which absorbed a large amount of money from the market by means of rights issues, disposed of their own company shares in order to pay for the shares allotted.

In order to cope with the deteriorating market situation occasioned by the over-supply of shares, the Government suspended capital increases from February to September of 1965. Ever since the removal of the suspension in September, the Capital Issue Committee has been screening applications for capital increases on the basis of three criteria: theoretical ex-rights price, dividend rate and ratio of earnings to capital.

A fundamental reform of capital increases is imperative. We are, therefore, proposing gradual adoption of the practice of offering stocks at near market price to shareholders. There are many arguments for and against such a practice.

Opponents consider that this practice will betray shareholders' expectations, and lead to sharp declines in stock prices, because shareholders are holding shares with the expectation that companies will allot new shares at par. The supporters of the practice, on the other hand, say that there will be no dilution of stockholders' equity because new shares are allotted to shareholders at a near market price. The supporters also point out the following merits to the new practice, and I completely agree with them.

1 Embarrassing over-supply condition of shares will be eliminated.
2 The debt-equity ratio will improve and the cost of capital for issuing companies can be lowered.
3 The lowering tendency of earnings per share will be prevented.
4 The stock market can function as a regulatory factor in adjusting the amount of stock offerings.
5 Managers will tend to pay more attention to the interests of shareholders.

C *Stock Investment Trusts as a Factor Exaggerating Market Price Fluctuations*

Stock Investment Trusts in Japan were re-established in 1951. From that time up untill 1965, subscriptions increased year after year, except for 1955. The total amount of outstanding principal increased from ¥59,519 million in 1955 to ¥1,185,897 million in 1965, an increase of about 20 times within ten years. In 1966, however, we witnessed a continuous decrease in principal amounts every month. (Table 12) Cancellations increased because of poor management of investment trust company portfolios and the sudden announcement of the rehabilitation program of Yamaichi Securities.

If you look at Table 12, you will notice that investment trust pushed the stock market further upward, backed by favorable subscriptions when the market was strong. Recently, however, they have become the biggest sellers in the market because investment trust companies have had to raise cash in preparation for cancellations. Investment trusts appear to have become disproportionately larger holders of shares as compared with other institutional buyers. Since investment trusts are like a whale in a small pond, they cannot move freely at present and if they act as they like, a market crash may take place.

In view of the fact that many series of trusts are selling below par, poor portfolio management is the focus of criticism. There were also improper relationships between trust management companies and their affiliated securities companies. Minimum requirements necessary to regain investors' confidence in investment trusts are (1) cutting of financial and personnel ties with securities companies and (2) full disclosure of their management portfolios.

H

TABLE 12 PRINCIPAL AND NET ASSETS OF STOCK INVESTMENT TRUSTS
(BOTH UNIT TRUSTS AND CLOSED END)

(in millions of yen)

Year or Month	Amount of Establishment	Principal at Par Prematurity Redemption	Principal at Par Outstanding Amount	Net Change of Outstanding Amount	Net Assets
1951 (July-Dec.)	13,300	707	12,592	12,592	14,056
1952	33,644	8,036	37,758	25,106	51,954
1953	59,982	17,153	76,446	38,688	78,434
1954	24,110	12,266	78,571	2,125	71,294
1955	26,381	31,792	59,519	(-)19,052	68,578
1956	51,431	27,163	67,748	8,229	83,671
1957	92,544	16,178	136,915	69,167	132,708
1958	106,412	25,741	209,695	72,780	242,937
1959	182,480	58,876	330,081	120,386	395,929
1960	362,066	87,945	604,202	274,121	768,955
1961	832,695	244,221	1,182,865	578,663	1,053,966
1962	430,935	336,334	1,263,306	80,441	1,099,633
1963	441,730	345,247	1,341,903	78,597	978,145
1964	452,490	384,532	1,370,594	28,691	989,084
1965	317,494	459,634	1,185,897	(-)134,694	908,161
1966					
Jan.	28,042	31,456	1,179,653	(-) 6,243	
Feb.	24,667	36,034	1,166,621	(-)13,032	
Mar.	24,404	48,086	1,139,311	(-)27,309	
Apr.	24,594	31,740	1,128,900	(-)10,411	
May	22,834	30,850	1,118,346	(-)10,523	
June	24,629	25,781	1,112,954	(-) 5,391	
July	26,593	26,844	1,106,980	(-) 5,974	
Aug.	22,665	26,241	1,089,741	(-)17,662	
Sept.	23,404	30,216	1,072,069	(-)17,667	
Oct.	23,737	25,057	1,057,036	(-)15,032	
Nov.	20,612	23,621	1,045,938	(-)11,097	

Source: *Zaikai Kansoku,* Tokyo, Nomura Securities Ltd.

It is also hoped that other institutional buyers such as pension funds will be developed, and thus play the role of a stable factor in the market in place of investment trusts.

D *Stock Market Supporting Organizations*

To revive the sluggish market, it was thought necessary to introduce some support measures. Despite the criticism that they may do more harm than good from the viewpoint of the free functioning of the market, such institutions as the Japan Joint Securities Corporation (since January, 1964) and the Japan Securities Holding Association (since January, 1965) were established for the purpose of pooling a portion of the shares floating in the market. Public confidence, however, continued to slide, and these institutions have purchased shares amounting to as much as ¥420 billion since they began their buying operations. In conclusion, I should like to explain briefly the characteristics of both institutions and the problems concerning their dissolution.

i *Japan Joint Securities Corporation (JJSC)*
At first, JJSC was organized through the sponsorship of 12 city banks, the Industrial Bank of Japan, the Long-term Credit Bank and four major securities companies, with an authorized capital of ¥10 billion (¥2,500 million was initially paid up). During the buying operations to protect the ¥1,200 line of the Dow Jones Index, JJSC included local banks, trust banks and life insurance companies, as well as medium class securities companies as shareholders, thus emerging as a large financial organization jointly sponsored by 119 of Japan's major financial institutions. At present, it has a paid-up capital of ¥30 billion and 15.3% of its capital is held by three banks (Industrial Bank of Japan, Fuji Bank, and Mitsubishi Bank), which took the initiative in establishing this institution.

JJSC owns stocks of 222 companies, amounting to 185 billion measured at purchase cost, an amount which is approximately 2% of the total market value of all stocks listed on the Tokyo Stock Exchange (1st section) as of the end of 1965. Approximately ¥100 billion was loaned by the Bank of Japan.

ii *The Japan Securities Holding Association (JSHA)*

JSHA was established with only securities companies as members. The association obtained loans amounting to ¥230 billion from the Bank of Japan through the Securities Financing Co., and shelved shares held by securities companies and investment trust companies, thus relieving them of financial burdens associated with their large holdings. Of the ¥230 billion, 50 billion was purchased from securities companies under repurchase agreements.

In April 1966, the release of JJSC and JSHA holdings was proposed by the Finance Committee of the Diet on the grounds that the demand-supply relationship in the stock market had almost returned to normal, and that the purpose of the two organizations had been virtually obtained. The Bank of Japan, that financed a substantial portion of the funds required to buy the holdings, agreed to the proposal. As a result, securities circles started to prepare for the liquidation, and during the subsequent months, liquidation sales took place on a small scale. As of the end of 1966, the sales totalled

for JJSC, 64,650,000 shares (13,500 million yen)
    or about 6 percent of the assets;
for JSHA, 22,250,000 shares (5,600 million yen)
    or about 3 percent of the assets.

However, the market response to such small liquidation was sufficiently adverse to cause a suspension of the scheduled sales. The feeling is now that the holdings should not be disposed of until the stock market regains full strength.

At the risk of being premature, the following suggestions have been voiced in regard to the future of JJSC:

1 Transform it into a private cooperative venture, by repaying the loans to the Bank of Japan, and giving it the characteristics of a mutual fund open to public subscription.

2 Give the 119 shareholders the right to take up JJSC holdings in proportion to their capital contribution, and then dissolve it.

3 Like IRI in Italy, make JJSC a sort of Government Holding Co.

As for JSHA, its members seem to be of the opinion that it should gradually unload its holdings by selling back to investment trusts, and placing the rest with institutions such as insurance companies.

Chart I. Breakdown of Corporate Sources of Funds in Percentage

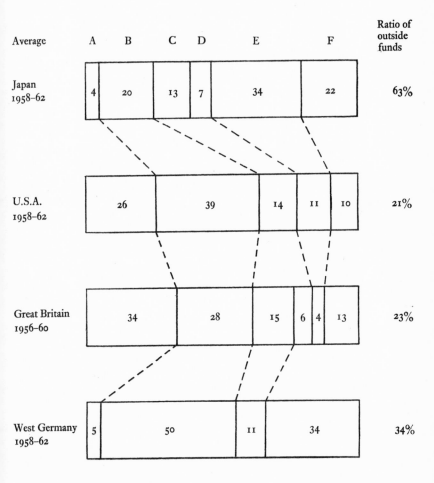

Source: Bank of Japan *Kokusai Hikaku Tokei* (International Comparison of Economic
Statistics)
Notes: A=Retained Earnings   B=Depreciation
         C=Stock   D=Bond
         E=Borrowings   F=Trade Payable

Chart II.
Call Rates and Yield at Issue (Corporate Bonds)

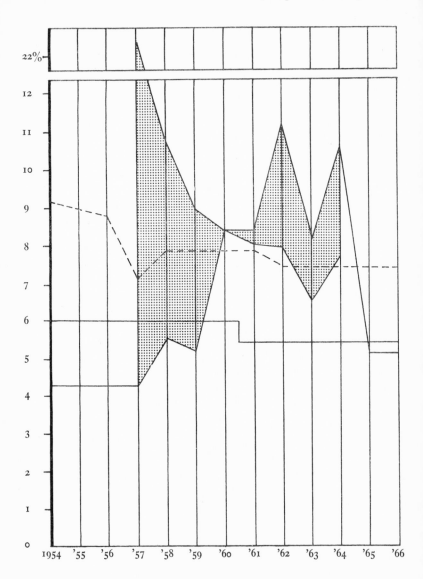

Source: Bank of Japan, *Economic Statistics*

CHAPTER VI

The Consumer Market in Japan

by George D. Johnston, Jr.

One barometrical device for determining economic development within the framework of a free market is consumption. What is the consumer looking for and what does he get? Are his wants satisfied? In this article Mr. Johnston answers these questions and analyzes consumer aspirations within the consumer market. The consumer market is the newest and most revolutionary aspect of the Japanese economy since World War II.

The Japanese consumer is now a demanding one; the author studies the demand and supply of consumer goods, particularly housing, food, clothing, transportation and leisure.

As the author points out, pre-war housing is considered by the Japanese as medieval; today the ordinary Japanese expects his own bathroom, and certain cooking and electrical appliances. The pre-war Japanese diet is insufficient for the modern Japanese, who has now become accustomed to such novelties as dairy products. The foreigner who comes back to Japan today after five years' absence immediately notes the fashion-consciousness that is spreading in the larger cities. The recent visits of such noteworthy fashion designers as Balmain and Cardin, and the success they have had, attest to this fact. In another area, more and more Japanese are buying their own cars, and this presents the three-fold problem of adequate parking, better roads and cheaper automobiles. Finally, the leisure boom, in terms of quantities spent, is astounding.

The author concludes the article by outlining future possible trends of these different aspects of the consumer market.

THE CONSUMER MARKET IN JAPAN

Housing—Food—Clothing—Transportation—Leisure—
Conclusion

What is the Japanese consumer looking for? What are his aspirations? How has he satisfied these aspirations? What aspirations does he yet have to satisfy?

In 1945 Japan was a defeated country, her industry and many of her cities were in ruins; since then, after a period of recovery and rebuilding, her economic growth has astonished the world. This growth has not occurred without some stresses and strains on society, without some imbalance in development and without some problems as yet unsolved. But it has placed Japan at the head of the international league: first in the manufacture of ships since 1956, first in the manufacture of motorcycles, first in the manufacture of cameras, second as producer of synthetic yarns, and second as producer of buses and trucks. Japan is third in the world in the production of chemical fertilizers, and third in the production of steel. Japan is fourth in the production of electric power and fourth in the manufacture of automobiles. Japan's export growth continues, and it is particularly strong in new types of manufactured products.

During this period, the Japanese people have become more and more urbanized. In 1965, 68% of the population lived in cities of 30,000 population or more. Concentrating more and more, the Japanese people are moving into the cities, with particular concentration in the three main urban areas of Tokyo-Yokohama, Osaka-Kobe-Kyoto, and Nagoya. These three areas account for almost 40 million people, which is a little more than one-third of the total population. People have switched from unpaid family work to paid employment. The difference between 1950 and 1964 shows a real drop in the number of people working in families and a real increase in paid employees. Many people have been moving from farm work to blue-collar work—practically the same picture is reflected in the increased number of people moving into the cities.

During this period, the average standard of living has greatly improved. The index of real wages has shown an increase of 60% since 1954, while average urban household expenditures, in real terms, increased by 52% between 1955 and 1964.

An international comparison made by Japan's Economic Planning Agency suggests that the real living standard of the average Japanese in 1962 was equal to that of the average West German in 1950 or the average Italian in 1955. This information, based on purchasing power, is a bit out of date, but it's an interesting comparison. In this growth period, the consumer has had some important aspirations realized, and is still waiting for some of his wishes to come true. Let us break them down, now, into five convenient and important categories: Housing, Food, Clothing, Transportation and Leisure.

Let us start with a breakdown of average family expenditures in urban households. In 1964, 38% went for food, 10% for housing (including durables), 5% for fuel and light, 12% for clothing, and 36% for other expenses.

Housing

Between 1955 and 1964, the percentage of expenditures spent on housing and durables rose from 6% to 10%. At the same time, the consumer has indicated that the problem that worries him most is housing. His worry about this has, in fact, risen in recent years. In a 1965 survey, 52% said that housing was one of the areas in most need of improvement. A large part of that increase in household expenditure on housing (from 6% to 10%) has, in fact, gone to increased rents. According to the consumer price index, rent increased by 141% in the nine-year period, without bringing equivalent benefits in terms of improved housing conditions. One major reason for consumer dissatisfaction is that quarters are cramped. The space per person is far smaller than in other developed countries. The average living space per household in Japan is 570 square feet; in the U.S., it is 1,000 feet. But, there are more people per household in Japan—4.4 in fact—so actual space per head is even less! The Japanese can live this way because they are used to it, but that does not mean they like it. 46% of dwelling areas in Tokyo are less than ten *tsubo*, or 35 square meters in size. A regular *danchi* (apartment housing area) apartment is just over ten *tsubo*, so that should be taken as a reasonable minimum standard for a small family.

For the worker, especially the white-collar worker employed in Tokyo, the major problem is the distance from his place of residence to his place of work. Many travel long miles and long hours to the office. They ride the commuter trains and subways, and if you ride them you will know the true meaning of the Japanese word *sushizume*—or packed together like rice in *sushi*.

The homes are small and far away, and they are also, in many cases, lacking in basic amenities. Though the *ofuro* (bath) is traditionally a daily institution, many homes do not have private baths; many—including some with baths—do not have running water. Another area of dissatisfaction in many homes is the state of sewage disposal; only 34% of homes in Tokyo have flush toilets; over the country as a whole, the figure is only 10%. On the other hand, Japanese homes have almost a surfeit of appliances. Sewing machines and electric washing machines are in general use. Television sets are literally everywhere. Appliances are the other side of the increase in household expenditures on housing noted earlier. This is one aspiration group that is relatively well satisfied, and is now arriving at the replacement stage. But it has created a few new problems, such as where to put the refrigerator when there is no room in the kitchen. This example points out how far the basic necessity of housing has lagged behind some of the least-needed luxuries.

The Government and some private building companies have built large apartment houses that have alleviated the basic problem of getting a roof over one's head. They offer good value for money, compared to many places. I am not talking now of the Western-style apartments, occupied mainly by foreigners, whose rents shock most new arrivals in Tokyo. Private companies and Government corporations help their employees with their housing problems by building dormitories and subsidizing housing costs. But a list 30 or 40 times longer than the number of apartments available is signed up when a new *danchi* is opened. The *danchi* themselves are still small, basic and bare, and are usually a long way from the center of town. Even among residents of *danchi* apartments,

80% of respondents in the same recent survey said they would move housing if they had the chance.

Why is the housing situation such a state? The first consideration in almost any problem in Japan is simply the number of people. Pressure on land is terrific in Tokyo, which has more people per square mile than any major western-type city in the world, and that pressure is increasing. A recent forecast anticipates a total population in Japan of 130 million by 1985, fully 90% of whom will be living in cities. Despite this pressure, the land is not efficiently used; 51% of the dwelling units in Tokyo are detached houses, 41% are of only one story.

Many small apartment houses have been built, and part of the building chain, connected with this style of building, tends to be made up of small firms, and is very conservative. It is not built to suit the modern consumer, but just to give him a roof. Such apartments, too, are very cramped for space. Japan's construction industry has been busy satisfying the needs of business and industry, and in this area has done an amazing job. But it has not yet really gotten around to housing. Yet although people claim to be dissatisfied with their housing, they do not spend much of their budget on it, relative to people in other countries—only 10% of monthly expenditures, including durables. The average American spends 20 to 25% on the same type of expenditures—25% of his salary every month. Actually, the Japanese consumer finds it difficult to move to better quarters. Demands far exceed supply, and he would have to spend significantly more to get only a little better housing.

But he has found he can improve his lot far more easily and at far less expense by improving what he has in his home, such as appliances and television—and what he does outside his home, such as going swimming or skiing. The average consumer, like many producers in Japan, is more concerned with less basic needs because they are so much easier to satisfy. But the problem still exists, and has a profound effect on many other facets of life. It must be solved, because land pressure is increasing all the time as more and more people move to the city. The *danchi* building program, and numerous studies of the problem, show that the Government is aware of it, and ways to alleviate it are beginning to be sought. The building companies are there and the techniques are there. Now they are building factories and offices; soon, they must build housing and apartments.

Food

The average Japanese urban household in 1964 spent 38% of its monthly expenditure on food. This had dropped from 47% in 1955. Though fewer people are worried about food than about housing, the consumer still has food on his mind. 41% of people named it a problem area in the 1965 survey, though it is not the area of concern it once was. In fact, a general increase in the quality and quantity of food has occurred, with the result that children are now taller than their parents, often noticeably so.

Consumption of meat of different kinds and of dairy products has increased especially fast. At the same time, two of the fastest growers have been coffee and beer, both of them enjoyment foods rather than nutrition foods. Modern Western foods have become part of the traditional pattern of menu planning. Bread has joined rice and noodles as a main course, or *shushoku;* meat has become more and more common as one of the side dishes, or *okazu.* Gradually, the concept of the main course itself is becoming blurred. Despite these improvements, the food the Japanese eat today is still inferior in quantity and quality to other advanced countries. The calory intake per person per day in Japan was 2,280 in 1963 (this is the last year we have been able to make a comparison);—considerably lower than countries like the U.S., U.K., France, Germany or Italy. Furthermore, the major portion of those Japanese calories is in vegetable foodstuffs. Animal foodstuffs still account for only 230 calories a day as part of the total calory intake of the Japanese consumer. Annual per-capita supply of meat in Japan is only about 1/13th of the U.S. figure. In fact, the Japanese diet is richer in non-essentials than in basic items. Thus, convenience foods have become a major market—foods new to the consumer, such as instant coffee, and instant versions of more traditional foods, such as *soba.*

Eating and drinking outside the home has continued to boom; there are now more than 240,000 restaurants, bars and coffee shops throughout Japan. While I know Engel's coefficient is often thought of as the mark of an advanced country, (on that basis Japan is far more advanced than Italy, 50% of whose average family expenditure still went for food in 1962), it can well be argued that a move upward in the proportion spent on food would benefit Japan—that is, if money were spent on basic foods of nutritional value and not just to meet increased prices.

The future will see a further Westernization of the diet pattern, and further improvement in the standard of basic nutrition. Here is a forecast recently made for 1985: to feed a population of 130 million, only 80% of present rice production will be sufficient, while meats and dairy products demands will be up to 880 and 660%, respectively, of the current level. At the same time, despite the continued efforts of the Government to push nutrition, it is clear that the consumer will demand more convenience and luxury in the food category, and be prepared to pay for it. We should look forward to and stimulate this as marketers, especially when nutrition can be combined with convenience.

Clothing

In 1955 and in 1964, 12% of the Japanese consumer's household budget was spent on clothing. Speaking generally, this is a well-covered area of aspiration, though a number of people still mention it as an area of their life that needs improvement. Western-style clothing, of course, predominates today. Nowadays, expenditures on Western-style clothes are over three times those for *kimono*. Many young women work, and office wear is Western wear. Strangely enough, however, the fastest growing category in clothing today in Japan is *kimono*. We think the reason for this is that women who work have money to spend, and many women today can afford more expensive and traditional *kimono* than could in years past. Japanese women seem to feel, however, that fashion and life are separate entities. They are conservative in their tastes, and their husbands are conservative, too. Their eyes have been trained by a long design tradition based on the *kimono*, and other concepts basically differ from Paris, London and Rome. This often seems to result in Western-style clothes that are not designed to fit or flatter the body.

But Japan's youth takes a less conservative approach. Young men lead the way, and many young women are now trying new modes and more startling clothes. As they grow older they may carry a consciousness of fashion with them, and their maturing tastes will, no doubt, be backed up by the next young generation with even more experimentation in fashion.

The high incidence of sewing machines in Japanese homes shows us another part of the fashion pattern. Many clothes are made at home, or custom-made by tailors and dressmakers. The ready-made industry is small, supplying approximately 15 percent of clothing needs, and because of that, fails to have much influence on fashion trends.

The personal care and accessories market, however, is highly developed. Shiseido, the leading Japanese cosmetics maker, has more than 600 products. Sales of costume jewelry, wristwatches and silk ties show that the consumer has shifted to the Western clothes that these things complement. Even men are active in this market, purchasing hair dryers and electric shavers by the thousands, and recently men's cosmetics. In fact, the consumer seems more accessory conscious than conscious of basic clothes design. With youth's growing interest in fashion trends and less conservative clothing, and with the probable growth of the ready-made industry, we can look for a more fashion-oriented mass market in the future.

Transportation

The number of passenger cars on Japanese roads increased from half a million in 1960 to 1.7 million in 1964; the figure for 1965 brings this total up to 2.2 million. In 1963, for the first time, the number of cars exceeded the number of motorcycles. Many of the cars are taxis, or company-owned vehicles, but the proportion of individually owned cars is growing and the word *"owner-driver"* has entered the Japanese language. Building expressways is a reflection of that boom on urban and interurban highways; this could not be seen in Japan before 1964. But the car boom is not yet on the same scale as that of appliances. The number of people per passenger car in Japan is still far greater than in any of the other major countries of the free world. Contrary to the impression one gets from looking at the elevated expressways, one of the chief problems facing the consumer in his quest for personal transportation is that most of the roads in Japan are unpaved, and the pace of road construction has been slower than the increase in the ownership of automobiles. Urban drivers already suffer from acute traffic congestion, due largely to inadequate road surfaces and inadequate road space. In crowded New York City, more than 35% of the land area is road surface; in Tokyo, only 13% of the land area is devoted to roads. This means that parking is a major problem too, and one cannot own a car in Tokyo unless one can provide off-street parking. All of this can only get worse as the number of cars increases.

Another deterrent to consumer satisfaction or consumer aspiration in this area is the generally high price of automobiles relative to income. A recent addition to the market—the Nissan Sunny—has upset the price scale considerably; its cost is ¥410,000, below the average for cars of its size and quality, and rumor has it that it may be the beginning of a price war in the 800 to 1,000 cc class. Another factor that should strengthen production and lower prices is the tendency to merger seen in the automotive market today. Japan has eleven individual manufacturers, but the Government feels it would be healthier to have a much smaller number of really big ones (witness the recent takeover of Nippon Prince). The consumer is avidly interested. There are some 20 motoring magazines on the stands today and motoring sections in many others, especially those aimed at young men. Auto-racing is a growing spectator and participation sport (witness Honda's entry into the Grand Prix races and the recently built Fuji Speedway). The automobile boom has significant implications for many aspects of life. Shopping habits may change if it grows easier to reach supermarkets. MITI predicts that the future growth of supermarkets will be confined almost entirely to the suburban or "dormitory" communities. Leisure activities may grow as it becomes easier and more comfortable to travel. The prospect of 30 million cars by 1985 is an awe-inspiring thought for city planners. It requires a massive rethinking regarding the relationship of various parts of the urban mix.

Here, too, is another case of attention being paid to non-essentials before basics are available. For the country as a whole, it looks as though cars will come before roads, and for the individual consumer a new car may well come before new shoes, new suits, or housing that he may really need.

Leisure

The leisure boom in Japan has been with us for a number of years. Participation activities of the modern age, such as skiing, swimming, golf and bowling, and spectator sports such as television, or baseball, or cycle-racing are very popular. It is difficult to realize how recently some of these activities developed on a mass scale. Japan now has the largest bowling center in the world. Five years ago, when the first alleys opened in Japan, Isluski predicted problems with high costs. Television was in only 8% of homes in 1958; today, television is in more than 90% of homes. In fact, the same Japanese whose house is too small and too far from work, whose food is too little and of too low quality, spent the largest time and money on leisure activities.

In the future, Japanese should have more leisure time due to a shorter work week, and, hopefully, shorter travel time to the office. The automobile will make him more mobile, and if the economy stands firm, he will have more money, some of which will, no doubt, go into leisure. Because of population density, the provision of facilities by public or private bodies will probably dictate the direction of leisure spending. As an example, the *pachinko* cult is basically due to urban youths not knowing what to do with their free time. The supply will be the stimulus of the demand, and there will by many opportunities for the marketer.

Conclusion

Let us draw some general conclusions. Housing is a recognized problem and an unsatisfied consumer aspiration. It is a difficult and expensive area to improve. The present supply is bad. The consumer, faced with bad supply and, no doubt, overwhelmed with the magnitude of the problem, prefers to spend his money on non-essential items that make his life more enjoyable or easy—on appliances, on entertainment, or on automobiles. With food, there are partly unrecognized problems—the low caloric intake, and its low animal foodstuff content. More money is available for food, but is being spent on luxuries and conveniences rather than on basic food items. The whole field is in a slow-change period that will probably find the consumer of the future having satisfied his basic dietary needs without losing out, perhaps, on either luxury or convenience.

Clothing is an area where there is fair satisfaction with the basics. There is, however, much more consumer desire for accessories and

I

cosmetics, and for having one more suit, or for a design trend that makes the most of a woman's physical assets. There will probably be no spectacular changes here, but the growth of the readymade industry should make the real difference in the general quality and quantity of clothing available to the average consumer in the future.

Automobiles are an enthusiastically recognized and as yet unsatisfied consumer aspiration. This area calls for considerably more expenditure by both the consumer and the Government. Paradoxically, money spent on automobiles and roads may make it more difficult to correct the basic needs of urban development, as in housing. The industry itself, as it grows, will create jobs and feed money into the economy.

Leisure is an aspiration which is recognized but still has room for further satisfaction. It should continue to grow as more free time becomes available and as incomes continue to rise. It could really boom if the pressures of urban development and housing do not throttle it.

The general conclusion that we can draw is that Japan's consumer boom has been largely due to the satisfaction of non-essential desires, sometimes at the expense of basic living needs, such as housing and food.

Part Three
BUSINESS

CHAPTER VII

Legal Aspects of Business in Japan

by Teisuke Akamatsu

This article studies the legal phenomenon in Japan and its relation to business. First, the author describes the organization of the courts, the jurisdictional breakdown and the legal professionals; those who assume that lawyers are legion, as in many Western countries, will be surprised to learn of the paucity of lawyers in Japan. The situation is not without remedy, since within the Japanese legal framework there exist "quasi-lawyers," dealing primarily with the administrative aspects of everyday legal necessities. Another difficulty for foreign businessmen is the almost total lack of Japanese legal experts for international transactions; this difficulty is coupled to the fact that no new foreign lawyers can be admitted to the Japanese bar.

Litigation is not appreciated by the Japanese and does not fit into their patterns of social ethics. Although this is changing, the use of courts is not as rampant and easy as in most Western countries.

In the second part of the article, the author studies certain problems of business transaction. He also points out typical Japanese attitudes towards contracts, which often surprise the foreigner, who has been used to a completely different meaning of the word "contract", and a different means of achieving a contract and putting it into force.

CHAPTER VII
LEGAL ASPECTS OF BUSINESS IN JAPAN

Court Organization—Legal Professionals (Lawyers, Other Experts, Law Graduates in Corporations, Liaison Lawyers)—Japanese Social Attitude Toward Law—Risk Taking and the Principle of Change of Circumstances—Enforcement of Contract (Notarial Deed, Immediate Compromise)—Joint-Venture Contract and Liquidated Damage—Effect of a Transaction that Violates Public Law.

Unlike some Western countries with a federal system, such as the United States of America or Switzerland, the Japanese legal system operates as a single jurisdiction. Its Constitution declares that the Diet is the "sole" law-making organ of the nation, and the Courts are vested with the "whole" judicial power.

Whether civil or criminal, the Japanese law which governs the public or private life of the people applies everywhere in Japan through its nationwide organization of the Courts.

THE JAPANESE COURT ORGANIZATION AS OF 1964

Court	No. of Courts	Judges	Jurisdiction
Supreme Court (*Saikō saibansho*)	1	15	Handles appeals from High Court.
High Court (*Kōtō saibansho*)	8	227	Handles mainly appeals from District Courts.
District Court (*Chihō saibansho*)	49	1,177	(1) Mainly first instance for all civil, criminal and administrative cases except Summary Court cases below.

(2) Appeals from Sum-
mary Courts.

Summary Court   570   715   The first instance for civil
(*Kan-i saibansho*)   cases involving less than
                                           ¥100,000 and minor
                                           criminal cases.

Family Court   49   341   Family relation cases and
(*Katei saibansho*)   juvenile   delinquency.

Total   677   2,475

These national courts have exclusive jurisdiction over all lawsuits in
Japan, and no other courts are allowed under the Japanese Constitution.

Legal Professionals

A Lawyers

In the United States of America with a population of about 180,000,000
there are about 250,000 lawyers, including judges and public prosecutors.
Although the Japanese population, 95,000,000, is about half that of the
U.S., the total number of lawyers registered with the Japanese Federation
of Bar Associations as of 1964 was about 7,000. Even if the number of
judges (about 2,500) and public prossecutors (about 1,000) are included,
the total number is not much more than 11,000.

In Switzerland with a population of about 6,000,000 there are about
2,500 lawyers. In West Germany with a population of about 60,000,000
there are about 20,000 lawyers. The international comparison of the
number of lawyers per 100,000 people is shown in the chart below.

	Population	No. of Lawyers	No. of Lawyers per 100,000
Japan	95,000,000	7,000	7
West Germany	60,000,000	20,000	33
Switzerland	6,000,000	2,500	42
U.S.A.	180,000,000	250,000	139

The shortage of Japanese lawyers is obvious, since their original role cannot be substituted. They are the only ones qualified to argue with competence before the Court, and give a high-level legal judgment which results from a strict examination system, from intensive apprenticeship in the Judicial Institute, from professional ethics and rules of the Bar.

The present selection system does not supply many lawyers. Out of some 10,000 applicants a year for the National Law Examination *(Shihō shiken)* (although national it is somewhat comparable to the State Bar Examination in the United States) only 400 (4%) pass. The examination is given only once a year, and most of the applicants repeat the attempt more than once, some even up to ten times. One cannot find such a difficult examination anywhere else in the world. The successful candidates enter into the Legal Training and Research Institute *(shihō kenshūjo)* of the Supreme Court for a two-year apprenticeship. About 400 graduates a year join, as they wish, one of the three branches of the legal profession: judge, public prosecutor or lawyer.

However well-trained they may be, such a small bar of some 7,000 lawyers is just too small for a nation of ninety-five million people. It stands to reason then that other kinds of experts must handle the vast volume of counseling, legal drafting, tax or patent work, etc., which falls within the scope of lawyers' practice.

b) Other Experts

There are some legal specialists of a sort in Japan. Among them are judicial scrivener, administration scrivener, patent agent, tax agent, public notary, etc.

The judicial scrivener *(shihōshoshi)* prepares any document to be filed with the court, such as pleading, brief, etc., for a nominal fee.

The administrative scrivener *(gyōseishoshi)* handles documents to be filed with the government, the patent agent *(benrishi)* those with the Patent Office, and the tax agent *(zeirishi)* those filed with the Tax Office.

The Japanese public notary *(kōshōnin)* is of rather a special character. Unlike his counterpart in Western countries, he acts not merely as witness for document-making, but sometimes as a public official with special authority, and he can even give the effect of court judgment to the papers he certifies. More will be said on his authority later.

The number of these experts as of 1962 was as follows;

Judicial scrivener	about	12,000
Administrative scrivener	"	7,000
Patent agent	"	1,200
Tax agent	"	12,000
Public notary	"	500
Total		32,700

Since there is, however, considerable overlapping of these qualifications, the actual total does not exceed 30,000.

c) Law Graduates in Corporations

There are in Japan about 15,000 new law graduates a year. It was mentioned above that only about 400 a year pass the National Law Examination. Most of the remaining graduates decide then to enter public or corporate offices. In various fields of specialization, they are the ones who handle the voluminous legal work that is usually done by lawyers in other countries. They lack professional training and the competence it gives, but in the particular field in which they are assigned to specialize, they obtain adequate skill in legal techniques. Their actual number cannot be determined because of the duplication in their roles as corporation employee and legal specialist, and the changes in their positions, from legal to non-legal and vice versa. It is this type of quasi-lawyer whom foreign businessmen will often encounter in business negotiations, contract drafting, corporate management, tax filing, or license application.

d) Liaison Lawyers (shōgai bengoshi)

The shortage of Japanese legal experts for international transactions is astonishing. Most Japanese lawyers limit their practice to domestic transactions, because of the language difficulty and the lack of familiarity with foreign law and society. On the other hand, since unlike some Western countries unauthorized practice is criminal under the Japanese Lawyer Law, neither are there many foreign-born lawyers practicing in Japan.

So far, the admission of alien lawyers has been very much restricted. During the Occupation period, the Japanese Government reluctantly admitted to the Japanese Bar without requiring them to take and pass the National Law Examination about 70 alien lawyers, most of whom were Americans. This abnormal admission system was abolished in 1955.

Out of the 70 alien lawyers so admitted, slightly less than 50 are actually registered as Associate Members *(junkaiin)* of the Japanese Bar. Except those practicing illegally, this is the number of foreign lawyers who have been playing a leading role in the international legal transactions carried out in Japan since the War. Furthermore, the Supreme Court Regulations limit the scope of practice of such Associated Members to cases in which their fellow-countrymen are a party, or cases concerning the law of their home country. For example, an American lawyer can handle only cases to which an American or British citizen is a party, or cases which concern Anglo-American law. He cannot legally handle any law case for, say, a Frenchman, unless the case concerns Anglo-American law.

There is no prospect that the Japanese Bar will again open the way to foreign lawyers in the near future, unless some mutual international agreement is arranged. Although the Japanese Lawyer Law does not require the alien lawyer to become a Japanese national, still he must be competent enough in the Japanese language and Japanese law to take the National Law Examination. We have already seen how difficult it is, even for Japanese applicants, to pass this examination!

In view of the paucity of liaison lawyers in Japan, the official legal exchange program and some private initiatives have recently sponsored exchanges between Japan and Europe and the United States. As a result, the number of Japanese lawyers who undertake the substantial task of qualifying for international transactions in terms of language, law and practice, is now slowly growing. At any rate, those actually engaged in international legal activities are not more than 50. Adding the 50 foreigners, we reach the total of 100 liaison lawyers, far too few to handle the vast volume of international business. This is a challenge to Japanese legal circles.

Japanese Social Attitude toward Law

In connection with the shortage of lawyers, the traditional attitude of rarely calling on lawyers needs to be mentioned. Japanese do not always like the clear-cut solution handed down in the courts. Many of them prefer social settlements like compromise *(wakai)* or conciliation *(chōtei)*.

This is partly because many feel that, keeping the medieval family structure in mind, the drastic victory or defeat in judicial litigation would interfere with the amicable relations between people, rather than protect their rights.

Most of these social settlements are conducted outside the courts by the relatives of the parties, or friends, or influential persons such as employer, policeman, mayor, senator, etc. This tendency is remarkable in domestic relations cases. For example, more than 90% of the domestic divorces (not international divorces) are so-called Agreement Divorces *(kyōgirikon)*. Such divorces take effect by the simple procedure of registering with the City or Ward Office upon mutual agreement, the same as for marriage. The case never goes into court. Although some cases *are* settled by mutual arrangement, most Agreement Divorces are more or less the products of compromise or conciliation, arranged by the parties' relatives, friends or superiors. Even in lawsuits, lawyers are not always used. According to recent statistics, in about 60% of the ordinary civil lawsuits in District Courts of the First Instance, one or both parties attended the hearings without lawyers.

We can, therefore, conclude that the role of legal experts other than lawyers and law graduates in Japanese corporations, as well as the Japanese traditional attitude toward litigation generally, bridge the gap between the legal demand and the shortage of lawyers. Recently, however, a sweeping change in the traditional attitude toward litigation has appeared. More and more people, especially in the business world, are becoming aware of the necessity for reasonable and enforceable solutions by means of the courts, rather than through amicable but non-enforceable settlement apart from the courts. This trend will aggravate court congestion as well as the shortage of legal professionals. A reform of the entire judicial system has been undertaken by the government, but it will take years. It must also be noted that the modern businessman might take a different view of the traditional way of settling disputes, now that effective measures are being adopted in the legal system, namely Court Compromise or Court Conciliation. These may turn out to be useful weapons for the enforcement of contracts, as we shall see later.

Selected Problems of Business Transactions

1 *Risk Taking and the Principle of Change-of-Circumstances*

The foreign businessman might encounter some inexplicable attitudes adopted by the Japanese businessman in regard to business negotiations. Among them are the request for postponement of a contract already concluded, or for a reduction of the price agreed upon, or even for rescission of the whole contract, without an appropriate reason.

Are there any legal grounds for such requests? The answer is generally no! Without mutual agreement or special provisions, the Japanese Civil Code does not allow the rescission of a contract. If the foreign party refuses, there is legally no way to accomplish the wish, unless the law grants permission to rescind under very special conditions; but the law does not usually provide such special permission. Japanese laws concerning private transactions are mainly derived from German law which is grounded on the rigid Western principle of *pacta sunt observanda* (contracts must be observed), and there is no legal basis for capricious change or rescission of contract.

However, a cautious non-Japanese businessman might note at least two exceptional situations under the Japanese legal system.

One is when the performance of contract has become impossible because of change of circumstances (impossibility). For example, X bought Y's house for ¥1 million. Before the new owner could take possession, the house was destroyed by fire. What about the money?

The other is when, because of a change of circumstances, the performance of the contract has become something quite different from what was contemplated by the parties at the time they signed the contract (frustration). For example Y rented X's house for ¥50 a month before the war. Because of post-war inflation the rent in the neighbouring residences went up to more than 10 times the former rent. Can X request Y to increase the price to ¥500 a month?

In the former case, since the performance of the contract is simply impossible, the only problem is, which party should bear the risk? If X is excused from paying the ¥1 million, Y takes the risk of fire. If X is not excused, he takes the risk. Therefore, the problem is termed by Japanese legal scholars as "risk taking."

In the latter case, although the purpose of the contract is frustrated by a change of circumstances (inflation), some methods are still feasible. Namely, if the rent price is increased to ¥500, the contract may still continue. This problem is considered under the so-called "principle of change of circumstances."

The system of risk taking is clearly defined in the Civil Code; hence, the solution depends on the interpretation of the law. However, the principle of change of circumstances is the product of Japanese court precedents. It should be noted that, although it is recognized as a principle, yet the Japanese courts usually do not recognize its application.

2 *Enforcement of Contract*

In dealing with Japanese enterprises, a foreign company ought to consider the prospect of litigation in case an extreme situation develops. In this regard, the congestion of the Japanese courts may sometimes appear almost hopeless. According to recent statistics, an ordinary civil lawsuit takes an average of one year in the District Court (first instance), a year and a half in the High Court (second instance) and two years in the Supreme Court (the last instance)—four and a half years in all. If a case is appealed to the Supreme Court level, it sometimes happens that the party has to wait as long as ten years to get the final judgment.

Furthermore, foreign businessmen as well as foreign lawyers are astonished to learn of the inefficacy of a court injunction handed down, for instance in case of violation of the protective measures for industrial property. Suppose, as agent for X, Y happens to hold X's written know-how. Losing trust in Y, X cancels the agency contract. If Y refuses to return the written know-how, contending that the cancellation was illegal, X is granted a court injunction against Y to the effect that Y must not dispose of the written know-how. If Y now, contrary to the court order, transfers the written know-how, he would probably come under the Anglo-American Contempt of Court system and land in jail. Since Japan lacks such a system, if the court injunction is ignored, X has no other immediate remedy than to file a lawsuit for damage, or, in a very unusual situation, to bring a criminal charge against Y. And this lawsuit will force X to sustain the long dreary struggle in the courts.

This is one of the points the modern movement for reform of the judicial system is trying to solve, but no concrete measures have been realized so far. Under these circumstances, the businessman may find it useful to equip the contract with certain formalities.

a) Notarial Deed *(kōseishōsho)*

A Japanese public notary *(kōshōnin)* has a more conspicuous function than the Western public notary. One of his main duties is to write the *kōseishōsho*. Although this is sometimes translated as "notarial deed," there is probably no counterpart in most Western countries. *Kōseishōsho* means not just the authentication of signature or seal affixed, or the acknowledgement of deed, but sometimes it has the effect of *res judicata,* that is, the same effect as a final judgment in court. Suppose a foreigner in Japan makes a loan to a friend. The friend agrees that the claim will be executed peremptorily against his property immediately if he fails to refund on time. This agreement can be made in the form of a protocol called *kōseishōsho* by a notary public. The foreigner does not need to file a lawsuit against his friend when the refund is not made. A court bailiff, upon the foreigner's request, will execute the claim on the appointed day against his friend's property, in virtue of the *kōseishōsho*, as if it were a confirmed court judgment.

This useful measure, however, can only be used for "the payment of a fixed sum of money, or the rendering of a fixed quantity of other fungibles or a negotiable instrument." Hence the *kōseishōsho* is not available for the execution of delivery of specific movables or immovables, or the execution when there is liability upon failure to express one's intention, etc. If a buyer X requests a seller Y to deliver, say, a boat, X cannot call in the public notary. For this an effective weapon has been prepared by the traditional measure for dispute settlement: compromise.

b) Immediate Compromise *(sokketsu wakai)*

Suppose that when buyer X paid for a boat, seller Y did not deliver it to X. After lengthy negotiations, Y eventually agreed to deliver on a fixed future date without resorting to a lawsuit. In this early stage of the dispute before the lawsuit, either party may apply for an "Immediate Compromise" procedure in the Court. The agreement to deliver the boat is put in the form of a protocol called "Compromise Protocol" *(wakaichōsho)*. X does not then need to file a lawsuit if Y again refuses to deliver the boat. Upon X's request, the court bailiff will immediately execute the delivery on the due date. The date of the Immediate Compromise is fixed usually two or three weeks after the application is filed in the Tokyo Summary Court. The parties are to attend only on that date, and the procedure usually does not take more than half a day.

Compromise is originally designated for dispute settlement, but it could serve for dispute prevention if conducted during the early stage of the dispute. This preventive use of the Immediate Compromise has been well accepted in Japanese practice. Foreign businessmen may find it advisable to use the Compromise Protocol for a part or for the whole of their business agreements on sales, house and land transactions, plant arrangement, etc.

3 *Joint-Venture Contract and Liquidated Damage*

An international contract establishing a joint-venture between a foreigner and a Japanese company is distinct from a contract of incorporation between promoters. Through the process of incorporation ranging from the opening of the promoters' meeting, the drafting of the Articles of Incorporation, the subscription of shares, to the registration of incorporation, the promoters form an organization which is an embryo of the future company. Because of the similarity between a partnership and an organization of promoters, both Japanese judicial precedents and scholars apply to the organization the provisions for Partnership Contract *(kumiaikeiyaku)*.

However, in the joint-venture contract, it does not seem that the parties form any organization until the procedure has progressed further; they will become promoters by entering a more specific contract of incorporation. Furthermore, the joint assets which a partnership generally holds are also lacking. When the joint-venture contract is just made, the relations between parties can as yet hardly be called a partnership. It is even questionable whether it is a contract in terms of enforceability: the date of establishment of the new company is uncertain, and the required formalities for incorporation—such as Articles of Incorporation, share subscriptions and constituent share-holder meetings—are usually not held. In fact, we may have only a declaration of the future program, or the contents of some previous arrangement, or at best the promise to incorporate in anticipation of the coming specific contract of incorporation.

Since the Japanese government exercises strict control over companies where a majority of the shares are held by foreigners, special control provisions for strengthening the foreign minority position are often sought in joint-venture operations. For example, the number of directors to be designated is usually agreed upon. Let us say that the joint-venture contract provides that X company and Y company each get half of the shares, but X is assigned three directors and Y two. Suppose that, after the incorporation of the new company, the parties quarrel, and Y insists on electing three directors instead of two. The election of directors is stopped, and the shareholders meeting is handicapped. There is no way, under the Japanese Commercial Code, to directly force Y to accept the number formerly agreed upon or to prevent Y from voting for the additional director it wants.

The agreement on the ratio of shareholders presents a similar problem. Suppose a joint-venture contract is concluded to the effect that X holds 60% of the new shares, and Y 40%. Later Y changes its mind, and insists on 50%. The contract is broken, but there is no direct way under Japanese law to force Y to respect the 60/40 ratio, other than to exercise indirect pressure by claiming damages. This is because the share subscription is generally a matter of agreement between a would-be shareholder (in this case Y) and the new company which, as a third person, is in no way subjected to any agreement between X and Y. And proof of damage is also difficult.

The parties to a joint-venture contract may be advised to insert a provision for "liquidated damage" against violation of contract; it is the only possible remedy at present, although indirect, under Japanese law. "Liquidated damage" is a promise of damage compensation or penalty. Once the contract is violated, the injured party will be immediately entitled to the liquidated damage, as provided, without bearing the burden of proof of liability and damage. In *Utano v. Gyokuzobo* (1922), the Japanese Court declared that the violating party was not excused from paying the amount of liquidated damage as contracted, even though it proved that it was not liable for the actual damage or that there was no damage. It has also been an established theory that the contract of liquidated damage restricts even the court from increasing or decreasing the amount agreed upon. Recently, more and more cautious parties use this preventive measure, even in international transactions.

4 Effect of a Transaction That Violates Public Law

Since the war, most important international contracts have been subject to the validation system under the Law Concerning Foreign Investment (FIL) and the Foreign Exchange and Foreign Trade Control Law (FETC), or sometimes to review under the Law concerning Prohibition of Private Monopoly and Assurance of Fair Trade, the so-called Anti-Trust Law. (Since a company, Japanese or foreign, can even now be legally established without referring to these laws, we will not consider in our discussion the incorporation problem.)

The legal effects of a transaction violating FIL or FETC laws or the Anti-Trust Law have been thoroughly studied by Japanese jurists. In general, both judicial precedents and legal scholars agree that any private transaction effected against the principles of "Public Policy" or "Faith and Trust" under the Civil Code is null and void. For example, in a case of a married man who promised to marry and support a woman, the court denied support to the woman plaintiff, applying the "Public Policy" device on the grounds that she knew of the man's married status. Also under the principle of "Faith and Trust," the court declared that a teacher who accepted the court compromise as to his discharge dispute cannot institute a new lawsuit for the same cause, even after a lapse of nine years.

However, there have been long disputes as to whether public or administrative laws could set up a standard independent from the Civil Code devices as to the validity of private transactions; and, if so, how and to what extent public laws could invalidate the transaction. Since *Tamaki v. Nakazawa* (1919), there have been a number of judicial precedents to the effect that an action taken in contravention of "police control" can be valid. In the above case, a customer of a rendez-vous house *(machiai)* which did not have a police license, was ordered to pay his fee. Most Japanese scholars agree with such a conclusion.

During the war, however, the Japanese government exercised strict control over the economy, and a number of cases appeared where any transaction effected in violation of the Economic Control laws *(keizai-tōseihōki)* was denied validity. The distinction between Police Control laws *(torishimarihōki)* and Economic Control laws thus became important as a validity standard for a private deal.

Although the Japanese Court has not clearly stated so far that FETC is under police-control, we have had several cases recently of private transactions effected in contravention of FETC, and yet being recognized as valid. In *Suzuki v. Japan* (1960), the claim of a promissory note drawn in Manchuria against the Japanese government, without FETC validation, was recognized in favor of a Japanese national. In *Greenhill Katō Trading Co. v. Shriro Trading Co.* (1960), the Court rejected the contention based on FETC violation, and granted an American company its sales claim against a Japanese company.

When the Anti-Trust Law was enacted in 1947, the overwhelming majority of Japanese legal scholars regarded the law as being an economic-control measure; hence, they denied the validity of private transactions effected in violation of the law. They reasoned that, if the violation transaction was valid, it could be enforceable with the result that the purport of the Anti-Trust Law would be utterly destroyed (Theory of Nullity). However, since the 1949 Amendment of the Anti-Trust Law, mitigating considerably the original trust control, some theories appeared supporting the validity of private transactions in contravention of the law. The reasoning is that the denial of validity is not merely unnecessary in regard to the effectiveness of the law, but harmful to the safety of private as well as business transactions (Theory of Validity).

Then came an epoch-making case, *Yokoi et al. v. Shirokiya* (1953) where a share acquisition in violation of the Anti-Trust Law was held valid. The court maintained that, although a transaction violating the Anti-Trust Law was generally void, the safety of business transactions *(torihiki no anzen)* must also be taken into consideration, after a violation has been committed. Thus the court granted the revival of voting power to the shareholders to whom the shares had been transferred in violation of the Anti-Trust Law.

On the basis of this judgment, some scholars declare that, once a contract is concluded in contravention of the Anti-Trust Law, the law does not always deny the results following the conditions of the contract,

K

although the Fair Trade Commission can still take some restrictive measures, apart from the problem of contract validity (Theory of Relative Nullity). Another school of the Relative-Nullity group states that, depending upon the content of specific provisions, an innocent violator may be excused from liability according to the Anti-Trust Law in so far as the validity of his private transaction is concerned. If, knowing the illegality, one offends against the Anti-Trust law, and such malicious intention is demonstrated in the transaction, his commitments cannot be valid. Thus the share acquisition in the above case could be invalidated, if the transferee knew of the illegality when making the transfer. This last school of thought would invalidate many of the transactions violating the law, but some special transactions, such as job duplication of corporation officials (Anti-Trust Law, Art. 13), transfer of business (Art. 16), or share acquisition in normal circumstances (Art. 10, 11, 14) could be supported as valid.

CHAPTER VIII

Accounting in Japan

by T. W. M. Teraoka

In the previous article, it was pointed out that what some may consider normal legal enforcement of contracts may not be normal in Japan. Accounting, too, has its local color, and the purpose of this article is to point it out. Two salient characteristics of accounting in Japan are the factors which determine the accounts presented, and the distorted use of auditors. The *raison-d'être* of an account in Japan is not necessarily to speak the truth about the outcome of business, but rather to keep the shareholders happy—at the risk of paying higher taxes—and to encourage the banks to continue producing loans. Legally, this "window-dressing" is not permissible, but it is nevertheless possible, a) because there is no regulation regarding the publishing of consolidated accounts and, b) the virtual control of auditors by management. The auditor, who is ensured a free hand in western countries, in Japan has access only to what management considers it necessary for him to see.

The author points out these discrepancies of accounting and then lists the methods used to "distort the image".

The second part of the article deals with Japanese accounting and how it affects international transactions. In general, the foreigners involved in joint ventures, or those emissaries from a foreign parent company to its Japanese subsidiary, are totally unaware of the "accounting in Japan phenomenon."

ACCOUNTING IN JAPAN

Accounting Methods—Dangers of Distortion—International Standards

In dealing with this subject, it is hard to decide which type of accounting to consider. Accounting for management? This would be easy, as I would simply give the grisly truth, therefore I shall not write about it. I might add, though, that the level of bookkeeping in Japan is not too bad so long as the right system is installed for the right company. Good accountants are not plentiful: put them on the right track, however, and they seldom go off the rails; so long as the out-of-the-ordinary circumstances are overcome, your accounts will be delivered to you. You must, however, beware of out-of-the-ordinary items, because in many cases they are ignored as not being "in the book of rules," and it would be loss of face for the accountant to admit that he does not know how to cope with them. Accounting for taxes? This would also be easy to explain since in a lot of companies every conceivable means of evasion appears to be taking place, relying on the gullibility and/or greenness of the tax inspectors, and the cunningness and/or downright untruthfulness of the explainor, plus of course a lot of luck.

To write about the methods attempted in the evasion of taxes would simply mean giving an explanation of every account in a balance sheet and profit and loss account, and telling you how to evade taxes. Our profession does not usually do this, even for a fee!

Accounting Methods

What about the other methods of accounting? I honestly believe that in most medium or large companies, the method of presentation of their financial statements is determined by their ultimate use, even if in some cases it means paying more taxes than are necessary. These are:

1 Accounts which are to be presented to banks or other financial
   institutions.
2 Accounts to be presented to the Shareholders.
3 Accounts to be sent overseas to the foreign partners or investors.

In these cases the aim is to produce good, steadily improving results
in order to keep up a steady dividend rate, no matter what has really
happened. Without the support of banks, financial institutions, shareholders and foreign participants, a vast majority of companies simply
could not exist. Take a look at most balance sheets in Japan; the loan
capital and short term loans are the largest and most important items
therein, and should the companies be denied such facilities, they would
quickly have to resort to the infamous moratorium of debts under court
order.

The accounts I refer to are those which are supposed to give information, not of the internal workings of companies, but information to outsiders. Many people grumble that accounts give historical costs only,
but to the investor, these are the only figures on which he can base his
judgment. Most people, before they give loans or invest in a company,
want to know the financial status of the company, and the only method is
by reviewing the latest financial statements. They have access to figures
published for Ministry of Finance or Japanese Securities Exchange
purposes, or they can go to credit investigation firms, or to the banks. But
can one rely on these figures?

How can companies conceal their actual financial position and get
away with it? It can be done quite easily at the moment in spite of the
Ministry of Finance report filing regulations, the Japanese Stock Exchange accounting regulations, the Japanese Commercial Code regulations on financial statement presentation, the appointment in every
kabushiki kaisha of at least one statutory auditor and the compulsory
audit of certain companies by independent public accountants. As in
many countries, the rules are there but the practice of conforming to
them is so loose that they might just as well not exist.

One of the greatest weaknesses of the enforcement of the above-
mentioned regulations in Japan, I feel, is due to the fact that consolidated
accounts need not be published; this in a country where—in spite of the
fact that people are told to think that the *zaibatsu* are no longer in existence—the majority of the large companies are interlocked through their

credit or banking systems or their directorates. In fact very few of even the larger Japanese firms consolidate their accounts for their own information; possibly they are ignorant of their own dangerous position. This situation, with subsidiary companies having different reporting dates, leaves it open for inter-company profits not divulged, the unloading of excess inventory on to a subsidiary, the transfer of redundant or inefficient personnel, the dangerous swapping of accommodation notes and the lengthening of credit terms between them.

Another weakness is the reliability of audit certificates in respect of published accounts. The main duty of an auditor is to certify that the accounts as signed by him represent a fair presentation of the company's state of affairs at any given date, and that the profit made during the period of his examination was also shown correctly. If he finds any material discrepancies he should draw attention to them in his report. The profession of public accounting is relatively new in Japan, and although there is excellent theoretical knowledge, this theory cannot always be put into practice. A principal reason for this is that the independent certified public accountant in Japan is not independent. In Japan at present the management of companies consider the hiring of outside accountants an infringement of their privacy. They do not want to give the auditor any information other than that which they think necessary. How many occasions have I come across the situation where my staff report that they have been unable to obtain certain information as the management consider such to be confidential! Of course it was confidential, that was the reason why we wanted to know about it! It then takes us a lot of explaining as to what an audit is before we get our answers. I am afraid in Japan the independent auditor, and indeed the Institute of Certified Public Accountants of Japan, have not yet achieved the strength and independence to stand up to management. As long as management can dictate the extent of an audit how can an unbiased set of accounts be published? Hence we have the wretched Sanyo Special Steel affair wherein the independent auditor was well aware of the situation and of certain malpractices of management several years before they became public, but took no action to bring the matters to the notice of the public in his reports due to the pressure of his clients, the management.

Another very vital reason for the weakness of an independent outside

audit is that there have been agreements for minimum audit fees nego-
tiated between the Institute of Certified Public Accountants in Japan and
the powerful Federation of Economic Organizations *(Keidanren)*. The
fees are based solely on the amount of capital of the company, which of
course bears very little relation to the size of the company. The companies
try to pay the minimum fees, and this obviously affects the time and scope
that the auditor can devote to such a job. Even auditors have to eat, and
although we love our work we cannot exist on that alone!

The office of statutory auditor is normally viewed as a sinecure, given
to an employee or officer for loyal services rendered. In many cases this
"auditor" has little or no knowledge of accounting, let alone auditing,
yet his duty under the Japanese Commercial Code is to examine the accounts of the company and certify to the shareholders that they are
correct. This position is an extremely dangerous one, and in my opinion
the appointment of such statutory auditors should be abolished.

We have the situation, then, whereby a company can "window-dress"
its accounts to suit its own purposes, and have few people question them
and many people rely on them. You can appreciate how dangerous this
can be, and in the case of a declining economic situation, the point must
come when there will be an explosion which will hurt everyone.

Dangers of Distortion

Now let us consider the various items which could be distorted in a
company's accounts, taking first the case of Japanese companies reporting
to Japanese shareholders only. As we have seen, the medium and larger
companies, apart from the relatively minor concealment of director and
staff fringe benefits, often maintain their books for most of the financial
accounting period on a fairly accurate basis. It is only towards the end
of the period when management compare the actual results with the
expected results that actions not in accordance with generally accepted
accounting procedures are adopted or contemplated. These are principally
to keep the shareholders happy, but also to keep their demands down.
The ideal is to show a steady upward trend of profits and at least maintain the rate of dividends. In good years, if a large profit is shown, the
shareholders naturally wish to participate by receiving large dividends.

The management usually tends to think "What will my position be next year if the profits do not continue to rise at the same rapid rate?" So in good years they try to show a fair increase, but not too much. "Let us keep some for a rainy day" is the usual attitude. Accordingly, they seek methods of decreasing profit.

The most common method appears to be over-providing for reserves such as depreciation. They will be disallowed for tax purposes, but the public will not know of this. This is a very popular dividend equilization account, which it is difficult for the layman to spot at once, especially with no comparative figures to refer to, and with the paucity of information on printed financial statements issued to shareholders. Another method is to juggle the reserve for price fluctuation on inventories which is based at present on a maximum of 6% of the total inventory. Here is a large amount of funds which can quite materially affect income.

Then comes the reserve for bad debts, another reserve which is allowed for tax purposes but often bears no relation to the actual position. This reserve, varying from 1.5% to 2% of total receivables, can also be manipulated according to the needs of the company. In order to reduce profit, the reserve can be "made up" to the amount necessary for tax purposes if it is under the tax amount allowable, or an excess amount, disallowable for tax purposes, can be made by management, again unknown to the public. Any queries can easily be answered by management to be their method of safeguarding the shareholders against future bad debts due to the uncertainty of the future economic position.

Another area is in retirement reserve allowances. It is customary in Japan to give up to one month's salary for each completed year of service to a retiring employee, even if the employee retires on his or her own request. This, in most foreigners' opinion, is a real liability to the company, and an accurately computed amount should be shown on the balance sheet and be provided for out of profits each year because, should the company close down, under the labour standard law in its acceptance of the company's working regulations, or the labour union agreement, the retirement allowances must be paid. The tax allowance amount of the reserve is fairly restricted, about one-half of the voluntary retirement rate, which in itself could be as low as 60% of the involuntary rate. Many companies endeavor to reserve more than the amount allowed for tax purposes, and if by chance their profits are too large they can increase this year's reserve amount—even if the proper charge is lower—because nobody can check on them.

These are four fairly easy but material areas in which profits can be manipulated downwards. There are other methods—we are discovering them daily!

What if profits are lower than what management think will satisfy their shareholders? This is a more serious position and accordingly more thought is given to it by management.

They can first apply their dividend equilization accounts previously mentioned; overprovision of depreciation is now remedied by not taking any depreciation at all this year—just to put matters right! The employees' retirement allowances are forgotten, the receivables for some reason have now promised to pay everything, and so no further charge to bad debts reserve is considered necessary—and yet this is probably just the time when such receivables should be reviewed more carefully—and lastly, the price fluctuation reserve was made for this purpose! Let it be said once again, that in many cases the companies are ready to pay taxes in order to maintain the confidence of their shareholders, the company's prestige, and—most important of all—to keep up their borrowing potential.

If these four reliable standbys are not enough to prop up the figures, there is a great variety of more sinister ways of boosting them, other than reducing the fringe benefits of the management and employees, which would be detrimental to the confidence of the same management and employees of the company. The following methods are deliberate misrepresentations, and much more dangerous than the other methods of "saving something for a rainy day," although none is to be condoned.

A favourite method is to increase sales—very simple if you have subsidiary companies which have different financial year endings, or unassociated but dependent agents or retail outlets.

Another method is using inventories. They are passed from one part of the country to another near the end of the financial period, but the cut-off dates are omitted from the books, so that the same goods are shown in the books in two places at the same time. Still another one—difficult even for the auditor to evaluate—is to forget obsolete and/or damaged goods lying for ages in the company's warehouses. When asked about such items the stock answer is "Of course they can be sold—at a profit too!" So they say, and they produce their best and most persuasive sales manager to extoll those optimistic future sales figures. What about showing inventory which is simply not in existence? This is a bit too dangerous for most companies who do not have complete control of their auditors, but it has been tried, not only in Japan.

Reduce liabilities, put off examining the purchased raw materials until they have all been used up in the manufacturing process, because it is quite a custom in Japan not to accept a purchase until it has been "examined" and found to be acceptable. There are so many ways of keeping the shareholders and the financial world happy.

International Standards

Let us now consider how accounts published in Japan stand up to translation into internationally accepted accounting principles. This is a problem we are constantly coming across in joint ventures—where the foreign partner provides only a technical representative who normally knows little about accounting, and the Japanese partners make sure that he is aware of this fact by mentioning many times the Japanese Commercial Code regulations—the foreign partner wants to know what is really going on from his country's accounting viewpoint. Then there is the parent company with a subsidiary in Japan, the parent has more control but once again it is the same as a mother trying to control her son's behavior 10,000 miles away. They quite often have no idea of the intricacies of Japanese presentation of financial statements and are really perplexed when they attempt to consolidate the figures arriving from Japan. In the same category are head offices with branches in Japan. Lastly come the innocent investors who purchase shares in Japan as well as on United States and European stock exchanges. They have to rely completely on published accounts and view them only from their knowledge of their country's methods of presentation. They are pretty well covered for their ADR or EDR purchases at the moment, as all issues to date have been accompanied by accounts audited and translated by firms of international accountants. The danger to the investor lies in purchasing shares quoted only in Japan with the relevant accounts issued in Japan only.

Our problem then is to translate the Japanese accounts into accounts in accordance with generally accepted accounting principles. Strangely enough the main areas requiring a large amount of adjustment or re-classification are those mentioned in the first part of this article.

We endeavor to straighten out the over- and under-depreciation of fixed assets over past years; we eliminate completely the price fluctuation reserve as it has no bearing in the accounts since it is not a reserve against any known contingency; we adjust the reserve for bad or doubtful receivables to a realistic figure, and we try to find out the real liability for retirement allowances. Having made these adjustments we are then faced with future deferred tax benefits and liabilities arising therefrom. Just these adjustments can change the whole picture of the original financial statements. Then we delve into the other items.

But one must bear in mind when reviewing a set of Japanese financial statements that in many cases the differences have been caused by adherence to the Japanese Commercial Code regulations on financial presentation—which underwent material alteration in 1964. It is obligatory for the accounts to be presented to the members in Annual General Meeting, by the allowances and restrictions of the Japanese tax regulations and by the business customs of Japan. Many of the changes to their accounts made under internationally accepted accounting principles puzzle the Japanese management, who sincerely believe that they have been producing normal accounts. They are exposed to the different approach and many are tending towards the implementation of such international standards of accounting. I firmly believe that in the future they will be achieved.

CHAPTER IX

Japanese Management Practices

by Ichirō Hattori

In the introduction to this essay, the author notes the usual foreigner's awe at the length and apparent inefficiency of the process of decision-making in a Japanese company.

The term "the group" has been used so often in the various sections of this book, that it appears to be the leitmotive of the work. Yet no study of Japanese social life or business practices can be undertaken without constant reference to "the group."

Similarly, within the context of decision-making, it is essential to realize that a decision is arrived at by consensus within "the group." This is a reality of Japanese business life: the individual does not act on his own initiative, but relates everything to the "the group".

To comprehend the process of group decision, the organization of the Japanese enterprise has to be perceived. The author deals successively with the structure of the organization and the system of promotion. The most important factor determining promotion and importance in the enterprise is the length of service. Nowhere else is the seniority system as prevalent and powerful as in Japan.

This system presents certain problems; one, which is becoming more evident as time passes is what the author calls "the generation gap." There definitely is a lack of communication between the new, post-war businessmen and the older generation, who harbor a different attitude toward work and company. This may be true not only in Japan, nevertheless, it is true particularly in Japan.

After having studied the organization and its attributes, the author analyzes the mechanics proper of decision-making.

JAPANESE MANAGEMENT PRACTICES

Organization (Structure, Promotion)—Problems of the Seniority System (Status Complication, Work Description, Generation Gap)—Mechanics of Decision-Making—Conclusion —Tables— Chart.

Business or industrial organizations in Japan have many practices which are very different from those in western countries. The most striking and interesting difference may be seen in the method of decision-making. A foreign businessman in Japan who has dealt with Japanese companies in the course of business knows this fact only too well. Somehow a decision is made within the Japanese company and communicated to him. But it is usually a slow process, which the western business mind often finds impossible to bear with. It is very difficult for him to challenge the decision, because he does not know who makes the decision. If he forcefully pushes the decision, he is surprised to find later that, for some reason or other for which nobody could be held responsible, the decision cannot be carried out in practice.

Some people say that these mysteries result from the fact that the Japanese company makes decisions by group. What is really meant by the group decision is not clear to everybody. I should like to show how this seemingly inefficient method of decision-making has come about, what the actual process is, and what can be done about it in the future.

Organization

A *Structure*

While it is dangerous to generalize, most Japanese industrial organizations have administrative units called *Bu, Ka* and *Kakari*. These are three levels in the management system as illustrated in Chart 1 (p. 165). The head or chief is called *chō* in Japanese, so *Bu-chō* may be the division or department manager, *Ka-chō*, the section chief, *Kakari-chō*, the assistant section chief. Above these administrative units is the corporate management consisting of the president and the directors. They are the management in the Western sense, but in Japan, where the lower units participate considerably in the process of decision-making, the body of people above *ka-chō* level should be regarded as the decision-making body. The concern of top level management and the concern of the administrative managers sometimes show intricate differences within this body: one is concerned with the overall interests of the company, and the other mainly with the performance of his own department. I shall return to this point later.

B *Promotion*

Let us now see how people are promoted within this hierarchy. For illustration I have shown the scale of standard promotion in my company in Chart I. This scale is applied to college graduates, clerks or engineers. They acquire the qualification to be recommended to *kakari-chō* when they have been with us for seven years. They acquire the qualification for *ka-chō* six years later, and after another seven years the qualification for *bu-chō*.

It is also helpful, in order to understand the people within a Japanese business organization, to know the relationship between their age and their monthly salary. This is shown in Table 1. Depending on the educational background, they are subject to different scales of salary. In each category a certain amount is added every year. The amount to be

TABLE I MODEL OF WAGE INCREASE AT DAINI SEIKO CO., 1966

Age	16	19	23	30	35	40
Graduate of Middle School	¥12,700	¥20,000	¥27,500	¥39,800	¥51,400	¥60,100
High School		15,140	27,500	43,500	54,500	63,400
College or University			26,500	52,000	65,000	80,000

Note: These are monthly amounts. In order to obtain the annual salary, about 60 percent must be added to these figures, since the company pays a bonus to employees twice a year.

TABLE 2. RELATION BETWEEN AVERAGE WAGE AND AVERAGE AGE

Size of firm by number of employees	300–500	501–1000	1001 and more
Title			
Kakari-chō (sub-section chief)			
Average age to qualify	33	33	36
Average monthly salary	¥38,000	¥35,000	¥48,000
Ka-chō (section chief)			
Average age to qualify	36	36	40
Average monthly salary	¥57,000	¥55,000	¥68,000
Bu-chō (department head)			
Average age to qualify	37	39	41
Average monthly salary	¥87,000	¥86,000	¥96,000

Source: Survey by the Tokyo Chamber of Commerce, 1963.

added is determined by the level of position of the individual, his length of service and his age. As we have already seen, promotion is very closely geared to age. Consequently, we can say that the salary is also determined by age and seniority. The industry average of promotion and salary is shown in Table 2. From this table we can see that the promotion is faster in smaller businesses (300–500 employees). For this very reason, a Japanese college graduate looking for a job is faced with a rather delicate choice. If he wants fast promotion, he should choose a smaller business, but a small business offers him less security and perhaps a narrower scope of work than larger ones. This choice is made even harder by the practice of life-time employment, and also by the common Japanese propensity to choose a company rather than a profession. There is no real loyalty to a profession. When a student comes to us, he is very flexible as to what he would like to do. But he is always very definite about wanting a job with us. Once employed, he stays with us until he is fifty-five, when he retires.

Having explained the Japanese industrial organization I should like to add some comments of my own. Sometimes people have misconceptions about this system of seniority. The system is so dominant today that we tend to think it has always been with us, is here today and therefore will be here in the future. In fact, if you look at the Meiji era, only 50 years ago, you will find many instances in which young and newly hired men were assigned to important tasks in the large business organizations such as Mitsui or Mitsubishi. As the supply of capable people overtook the growth of the economy, the system of seniority has gradually been established. For this reason, my opinion is that we should not regard this system as the product of an *a priori* mentality of the Japanese, but it should be regarded as the product of particular social and economic conditions of the present time. Just as the speed limit and traffic lights ensure smooth traffic, this system maximizes the satisfaction of employees and, at least until now, it has also been the best way to ensure a smooth flow of work within the organization.

Problems of the Seniority System

A *Status Complication*

Under the seniority system, it is difficult for the corporate management to delegate authority downwards. By the very nature of the system, authority has to be assigned by seniority, not by capability. Under this system people get promoted and given greater authority when their turn comes. If this system is strictly observed, people lose their drive for work, and the organization will certainly become inefficient. It is necessary, therefore, to give to certain capable people positions which their seniority does not permit. This contradiction leads to a great complication of status structure within organizations. You meet people with titles like sub-manager, assistant manager or vice manager. They are all managers, and, as such, their degree of responsibility within the company should be the same. By the difference in their titles, though, the difference in their seniority is accounted for.

B *Work Description*

It is difficult to define the job of each manager. We just cannot think of a situation in which we define the work first and then find people to fit it. Whether capable or not you have to try to promote people from within the company. For this reason the description of work in Japanese companies is usually very vague, in order to allow sufficient room for *ad hoc* judgment. It show only the kinds of work to be assigned to each section. It almost never specifies work or responsibility of individuals, nor does it tell you how the authority should be divided between the superior and his subordinate.

Another consequence of promoting people only from within is that the managers sometimes tend to be independent, expecting little leadership or instruction from the corporate management. Regardless of many efforts to choose top executives solely on the basis of their capability, it is still seniority which carries the heaviest weight. Consequently, many of the department managers will have worked with their company for thirty years or more before they come up in the waiting list for directorship. The managers and their superior, the director, by this time know equally well all operations of the company—after all they have been with the same company for a very long time, and it seems that there is little one can add to one's knowledge after having been in the same place for thirty years or more. Under these circumstances, what managers expect from their superior is not leadership but only the authorization of their plans so that they can push them through the admistrative channels within the company.

c *Generation Gap*

There is another very important fact which hinders communication between the different levels of management. This is the so-called generation gap, a conflict between entirely different ways of thinking and attitude toward work and company.

The mentality of young people today is entirely different from that of twenty years ago. It is true, of course, that the contemporary culture in any country is different from that of fifty years ago, and a certain continuity exists through the changing culture. In the case of Japan, however, the change was caused by a sudden destruction of this continuity after the war, by a drastic reform of the system as well as the policy of education. The once commonly accepted norms of conduct by which the superior could give orders to his subordinates are no longer valid to today's younger generation, whose norms of conduct have a heavy propensity toward pragmatism.

The fact remains, however, that under the system of seniority and life-time employment, people in an organization share the feeling of security through togetherness. For them, the exclusion from the process of decision-making would mean the denial of a feeling of security.

Mechanics of Decision-Making

The actual mechanics of decision-making depend on a document called *ringisho*. Plans are stated on this document to be circulated to related departments and then to be submitted to the top executives for their authorization. Due to the problems we have already discussed, this process is not a simple matter. If a department manager wants to get an authorization, he usually asks one of his subordinates to write it for him. Since writing a formal document in Japanese is not as simple as having one written in English by way of dictation and typing, managers cannot spend their own time drafting documents. If a manager asks his subordinate, the process automatically involves the subordinate in the decision-making process. Because the man whom the manager asks to write a *ringisho* is not just a typist or his secretary, but usually his direct subordinate, this person may have his own view about the matter. The subordinate's idea may be based on his own philosophy characteristic of his own generation. If this is the case, the manager must be ready to spend a good deal of his time for adjustment. Even though this adjustment sometimes ends up in a bitter argument and hostile silence, this is a very necessary step to get things going. If a *bu-chō* asks his *ka-chō* to write the plan, and the *ka-chō* in turn asks the *kakari-chō*, the same procedure is repeated twice involving more people in the process. This is why one must regard all the people above *ka-chō* as the decision-making body. In this way a lot of energy is consumed before the document is even circulated. (Chart 1. p. 165)

When the document is ready for circulation, there are usually questions and objections from the related departments. To avoid these questions, the department manager who initiated the plan calls a conference of related departments before the document goes out. Each department sends one *bu-chō*, one *ka-chō* and perhaps two *kakari-chō*. If there are four departments, about 20 people will attend. As the Japanese say "too many captains will guide the boat to the top of a mountain," and conferences in this manner are very time consuming. When the circulation is completed, probably fifteen or twenty seals of managers and their assistants appear on the *ringisho*. This document finally goes up to the top executives for their authorization. When the plan is okayed by them, the manager who initiated the plan is given the authority to go ahead with it. The financial department will put aside money for him and the personnel department will provide people. Therefore, this *ringisho* should be regarded as the only formal way to delegate authority downwards. We can say that authority in Japanese companies is delegated on an *ad hoc* basis by *ringisho*.

It is important to note that the implicit function of *ringisho* is to involve all related departments in this decision-making process, and to have them fall in line. If a manager has enough authority over the managers of other departments, he could simplify the process a great deal. He could, for instance, avoid the lengthy conference, and this is where the difference of seniority plays an intricate role.

Under these circumstances, it is a very delicate problem for corporate management to achieve correct distribution of the decision-making authority. With all the authority concentrated at the top, the top executives will be overwhelmed by reports and *ringisho* and will have no time for their own work. On the other hand, if they loosen control too much, they will find themselves in a vacuum without information about their own company. To find a good balance between the two extremes requires a special skill which only people with long experience with the company can acquire. To manage a seniority organization efficiently really needs a senior man.

In summary, I would like to say that the process of asking for authorization being the only formal way of delegating authority, decisions are made not on the basis of an explicit recognition of the function of individual persons, but are likely to be made as a result of a complicated interaction between the corporate management and the administrative units, the former holding the right to authorize and the latter holding the initiative to plan.

Conclusion

Having discussed the facts and problems of Japanese business organizations as well as the actual process of decision-making, I would like to try to examine whether this method of decision-making can be justified today. Until now it has had good reasons to exist. In a period in which business is going smoothly, there is no need for major changes in business policy. Why should you not run the business by encouraging your managers to plan for you? Particularly if their morale is improved thereby. This has been the case for the past twenty years in the Japanese economy. It was a period in which the direction of business was very clear to everybody. Everybody knew that the plan for growth and expansion was a good one. In such times the inefficiency caused by this decision-making process is comparatively small. It can be more than offset by efficiency in execution as the result of participation. We must remember, however, that this might not be delegation of authority in its true sense. Many companies claim good results from delegating authority to their lower administrative units. I suspect very much that it is just the delegation of the right to plan, retaining the process of authorization for the top executives. In any event, it was all right for that particular time of the Japanese economy when everybody was planning for expansion.

Today, the situation looks entirely different. The corporate managements have to initiate major changes in many instances, changes which greatly affect the routine operations of particular departments. Today, and in the period to come, the corporate management and the administrative managers should recognize the special functions of each. The corporate management should use more time for determining policies rather than authorizing only plans initiated by the lower units, and the administrative units should be delegated authority in the right way, so that they can act more quickly without the lengthy process of circulation and authorization, as long as they are in line with set company policies.

There are many problems to be overcome, and there is no quick-effect medicine for these problems. The duty of corporate management today is to have a firm recognition of the need for improvement, not for the sake of just changing the system, but they must recognize that the growth of the economy of Japan depends on the performance of each individual company, and that the growth achieved through the prosperity of each individual firm will automatically alter the situation and remove all the difficulties.

Chart I. Organizational Structure

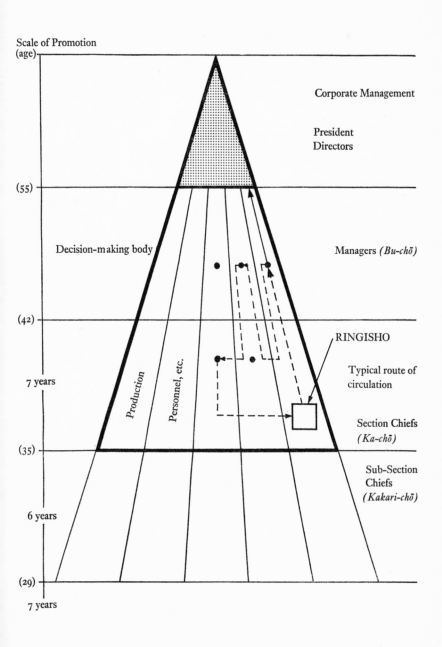

Scale of Promotion
(age)

Corporate Management

President
Directors

(55)

Decision-making body

Managers *(Bu-chō)*

(42)

RINGISHO

7 years

Typical route of
circulation

Production

Personnel, etc.

Section Chiefs
(Ka-chō)

(35)

Sub-Section
Chiefs
(Kakari-chō)

6 years

(29)

7 years

Re-Organization in Japanese Enterprises

by Susumu Takamiya

The final article continues the analysis of management practices in Japan. The author describes the differences of business organization in Japan and the West: the West stresses the work aspect, whereas Japan emphasizes the human aspect. Again, it is underlined that a business in Japan is not only an economic phenomenon, but also a social phenomenon.

Co-operation is the secret of success, while individualism has no place in this tightly knit pattern of behavior. In the West, responsibility is commensurate with authority, whereas in Japan, responsibility is synonymous with obligation.

However, the author notes that times have changed, and so have business attitudes. The old management philosophy of paternalism and internal harmony is on the wane, and a newer, more dynamic philosophy has to be sought out. Indeed, there are numerous proposals for reform which are currently being studied.

RE-ORGANIZATION IN JAPANESE ENTERPRISES

Business Organization—Ringi System—Other Reforms—
Top Management—Notes

Two examples will help focus the problem:
1 Last Summer, after a speech I gave at the London Institute of Directors, an auditor stated that the biggest difficulty in starting business with a Japanese firm was to find out exactly with whom to speak in the company.
2 The second example was found in the May 17, 1964 issue of the *Sunday Times Magazine.* A survey of Japanese business started as follows:

"In Japan today, businessmen spend their lunch hour practicing golf on skyscraper roofs, leave scores of letters unanswered, arrange three-quarters of the marriages of their staff, and . . . get ships built much faster and more cheaply than in Europe. Is the boom built on sweated labour? Are the Japanese really efficient? Can Britain hope to compete?"[1]

Both observations are penetrating ones, and bring us face-to-face with the problem of authority and responsibility, particularly that of decision-making, one of the most vital issues of present-day Japanese management. In fact, it is the basic problem of Japanese business organizations.

Business Organization

A business organization has two aspects: it organizes people and it organizes work; both must be integrated in order to achieve a going concern. Japan has traditionally placed emphasis on the human aspect, whereas in the West companies stress the work aspect. It could probably be said that the Western type of business organization should give more direct consideration to the human side of its work-oriented structure. Western business executives are often at a loss, though, when, coming to Japan, they wonder with whom to make the initial contact in an organization where the logically organized work-structures are far from obvious.

In Japan, the business organization is not a mere mechanism geared to work; it is a *Gemeinschaft,* a human group marked as a specific and lasting entity by its own spirit, life and history. Individual employees are an integral and organic part of the organization, and their work behavior is characterized by group behavior; although a particular phase of the work may be the performance of an individual, it is recognized only as part of the total group behavior. Within such a context, management developed its paternalism, so strikingly exemplified by the permanent or life-long employment practice, which in turn strengthened the industrial *Gemeinschaft.*

Consequently, the sense of identification with, or belonging to, the company is very strong, and since work is performed by the group, the need of establishing and identifying specific authority and responsibility of the individual in regard to work performance is not felt acutely. In fact the lack of work structure is made up for by strong group consciousness. It is, of course, possible that individual efficiency may be low, but the total performance of the company resulting from collective behavior is high; the merits of cooperation have more than made up for the disadvantage of individual inefficiencies. This is the key to the impressive growth of many Japanese enterprises.

The article in the *Sunday Times Magazine* went on to say:

> "Paternalism makes for a sluggishness and inefficiency quite astonishing in the land of economic miracles. It takes hours, days or months to obtain a definite answer on quite simple matters. For instance, when I asked at the Honda Motor Co. for permission to visit the factory, the executive replied that it would be necessary to write to their Hamburg office for approval!"[2]

Such a case is not out of the ordinary in Japan! But it should not be looked at by itself. The reason for the miraculous development of some Japanese firms is found in the strength of the cooperation resulting from their human organization. This point is clearly seen when one considers the workings of authority and responsibility in a Japanese firm.

A principle of Western organization is that responsibility must be commensurate with authority; but the principle is valid only as far as the individual on the job is concerned. The Japanese principle, on the contrary, calls for unlimited responsibility and limited authority. In this sense responsibility is synonymous with obligation, the obligation to contribute to the company as a member of the *Gemeinschaft*. This characteristic is often admired by foreigners, and much envied, especially by American businessmen. However, their Japanese counterparts are much concerned about another aspect, namely the difficulty of defining responsibility and authority in terms of individual jobs. An urgent need is felt to come up with a rational structure of work organization, which would define the authority and responsibility delegated to the individual in the execution of his specific job.

Ringi System

These organizational problems are best exemplified in a typically Japanese management practice called the *ringi* system. The Japanese term is composed of two ideograms; the first one, *rin*, means in the context that subordinates submit a proposal to their superiors, and the second one, *gi*, means discussion. Since in the traditional Japanese business organization formal authority for making decisions is concentrated in the hands of the chief executive, the president of the company, those in charge of a specific task cannot make independent decisions regarding their own job. They are expected to write a description of the matter in the form of a proposal which is then coordinated with related departments, and finally submitted for decision to the president. Only then may the proposal be acted upon. This process of decision-making involves in fact a large number of people. The original written document, *ringisho*, is passed around to all concerned; each affixes his seal on the document as evidence that he has seen it and passes it on to the next department. A head of department or section who disagrees usually adds his own opinion besides stamping his seal. This procedure in itself is probably not peculiar to Japanese management as a method of communication and decision in a centralized organization.[3] It is, however, characteristically Japanese in its intimate relation to group decision-making.

The point is best made by presenting the merits and demerits of the system. It has the very definite advantage of being initially written by someone directly in charge of the matter, normally a member of middle management. It is therefore an expression of so-called "bottom-up" management, allowing for participation in decision-making within a formally centralized organization.

It may even go as far as *mekura-ban* or "blind stamping," when the president affixes his seal without checking the contents of the document, feeling that the matter is not so important or that the proposal contains no error, after having been stamped by all concerned. Actually this amounts to an informal delegation of authority, whereby the formally centralized organization gets for all practical purposes the benefits of decentralization. It presupposes, however, that an experienced president sorts out instinctively the unsound *ringisho*. In any case the *ringi* system is useful, be it only as a record to be filed.

The demerits of the system can be listed readily:

1 It is apt to degenerate into mere red tape, the curse of bureaucracy. Emphasis tends to be placed on the techniques of documentation in order to obtain the top man's approval. The document further tends to be passed around to too many offices, accumulating a large number of seals. In the case of a certain large company, as many as 30 seals had to be obtained for one single *ringisho ;* it often took one month before it reached the president.

2 The system permits evasion of responsibliity. Usually it is far from clear what all these seals really mean, and to what extent or in what respect the people affixing them assume responsibility.

3 The procedure tends to dilute the top leadership concerning overall policy-making, since *ringi* decisions by the president regard individual operations.

  The criticism is often heard that Japanese top management does not exercise leadership as it should.

4 The president's approval by the *ringi* system is tantamount to prior supervision of the subordinate's work, which tends to give the false impression that supervision is completed and that the follow-up is not needed anymore. For the same reason, subordinates will neglect the necessary reporting to their superiors.

In short, the *ringi* system is a formalized process of group decision-making; as such it symbolizes insufficient definition of the individual's area within the group, as well as of the authority and responsibility attached to each individual job. It is a drag on the needed reforms of these functions.

Efforts are now made to revise or even to eliminate the *ringisho*. The first approach consists in distinguishing two types formerly processed indiscriminately: the *ringisho* for coordination and decision-making, and the other as a means of communication. In the latter case, copies would be distributed after approval has been obtained. In the former case, the number of seals would be reduced to a necessary minimum and a time limit would be set for each affixing of the seal; only important matters would, however, be processed and require the president's approval. In effect, it would formalize the delegation of authority and require the definition of matters that need top approval.

But such a reform would not yet eliminate the defects of the *ringi* system; some large companies are now boldly abolishing it! It means for these firms to define clearly the authority and responsibility attached to each position, encourage individual decision-making, determine the relations between line and staff, and adopt modern methods of communications. The trend is off to a good start. Recently, I conducted a seminar on the *ringi* system, sponsored by the Nippon Office Management Association; discussions centered around actual cases of companies that have recently abolished the system, namely Teijin, Asahi Chemicals, Hokuriku Electric Power, and Nippon Light Metal. Excellent results were acknowledged. There is growing recognition that the central problem of Japanese business organization is the crying need for establishing a rational work structure and integrating it within the corporate human organization. The abolition of the *ringi* system is a bold step in that direction.

Other Reforms

In 1963, I conducted by questionnaire a survey of 100 large companies.[4] Of these 54 reported that they had a job analysis program, and 21 reported, that they were planning one; 38 also reported that they had formally defined responsibility and authority. 64 firms stated that their top management was making the decisions concerning the work to be executed by the departments; among the remaining companies, however, 29 answered that such decisions were delegated to the department heads. In regard to the lowest level of decision-making, 20 reported the assistant section heads *(kakari-chō)*, 40 reported the section heads *(ka-chō)*, and 19 reported the department heads *(bu-chō)*. It is further interesting to note that 34 out of the 100 firms had adopted the organization structure by product divisions, and 24 of these had at the same time established decentralized profit centers. Line-and-staff organization is featured in 77 firms; this is a most remarkable development when one considers that fifteen years ago the concept was almost unknown in Japan. Most large firms nowadays have adopted the system and publicize their organization charts of the line-and-staff type. One may, however, still wonder whether the actual organization follows the chart.

As the organization of the work is gradually established and the individual's authority and responsibility become clear, a corresponding change has appeared in the traditional seniority-based personnel policy in Japan. A new development here is a personnel policy giving more consideration to the development of personal ability. The general trend in Japan in this respect is that, in work situations, such ability is increasingly emphasized and enterprises try to adopt the system of promotion on the basis of ability, while for wage administration the traditional policy of seniority is retained. In other words, wages and work are separately administered, with a view to maintaining the stability of the life of employees in wage administration based on seniority, and to ensure the increase of the productivity in work situations by promotion based on individual ability. This is a form of integration of the work structure into human organization, which is now progressing in many Japanese companies. Although these policies seem contradictory, they are integrated by the Japanese way of thinking, which can harmonize contradictory matters.

Recently, on the other hand, *Gemeinschaft*-type strength of Japanese management is beginning to fade. Since World War II individualistic thoughts have begun to dominate the behavior of the younger generation, gradually weakening the strong pre-war sense of identification with the company.

The *Gemeinschaft*-like cooperative spirit of the organization which once made up for the defects in the inefficient work structure has begun to weaken. Management will lose its effectiveness unless a rational work structure can be constructed to make up for the gap which is opening between the human organization and the work organization.

At the same time, Japanese industry is now being forced to motivate group consciousness of employees through the new concept of social responsibility of enterprises.

It is not enough to merely define authority and responsibility for individual employees. Studies are now being made to implement the new concept of management by objectives, by setting specific objectives for fullfilling the responsibilities of individual employees.

In the area of wage administration, too, efforts to introduce a job-based wage system would expedite the new trend to integrate it into the traditional seniority-based wage system, which also means harmonizing contradictory matters.

Top Management

Top management itself is affected by the trend toward change. The postwar Commercial Code prescribes an American-style Board of Directors, but very few large firms in Japan offer to outsiders the position of director; the new institution, therefore, has not meant progress. But another institution, which I myself proposed in my book *The Organizational Reform of Enterprises,* published in 1947, has been widely adopted— the *jōmukai,* now the group decision-making device at top management level. It consists of managing directors, and the president is its chairman. The managing directors function in an advisory capacity to the president. The president does his decision-making by group discussions with his managing directors in this meeting. Its most important characteristic is that the members are professional managers. In postwar years, the separation between management and ownership in big corporations has been spread in Japan by the dissolution of the *zaibatsu* and the democratization of the stock market; professional managers came thereby to the fore. In recent years, they have displayed an extraordinary zeal for qualititative improvement, prompted as they are by the necessity of coping with the impact of trade liberalization on the international level,

M

and on the domestic scene with labor shortage and rising wages. They now work under the imperative need to match by present qualitative development the past quantitative growth of the economy.

The task is most delicate. Recently, *Keizai Dōyūkai* (Japan Management Association), a group of progressive top executives, outlined the challenge.

"Traditionally, the outstanding features of Japanese management have been related to the concepts of internal harmony and paternalism. These values were the core of management philosophy, and the main factors responsible for the development of our enterprises. They were also quite rational in the sense that they were consonant with generally accepted social values. Today, however, this value system is undergoing a drastic change, and the concept of total allegiance to the company is criticized. It is time to look for a new philosophy of management."[5]

This new philosophy should attribute greater importance to individual skill and knowledge as the link between the firm and its employees; the delegation of authority should be implemented accordingly. But, though paternalistic management is usually associated with easy-going and obscure responsibility, the nature of the corporate system has, on the other hand, desirable effects on employee morale and loyalty. Internal harmony gains increasing relevance if it is fostered as a means to facilitate the cohesion of a group with diverse and superior talents working toward a common goal. The task is how to integrate the job system and the corporate system.

Notes:
[1] May 17, 1964 issue of the *Sunday Times Magazine*, p. 7.
[2] *Ibid.*, p. 12.
[3] In a private conversation with Prof. Pigors of M.I.T., he pointed out that a similar method was prevalent in the U.S. around the end of the last century.
[4] S. Takamiya, "Research of 100 Big Companies in Japan," *Chūō Kōron*, 1963.
[5] Keizai Dōyukai, *New Philosophy of Japanese Management*, Tokyo, 1964.

Statistical Appendix

Statistical Appendix

Compiled and edited by Kinichiro Saito

Contents

1 : JAPAN'S LABOR FORCE BY INDUSTRY

Japan was already an industrial power before World War II, but nothing like the industrial giant she is today.

The rapidity of the change can be shown by changes in the past twenty years in the distribution of the labor force by type of industry.

In 1955, 41 perccnt of the labor force in Japan were in primary industry, and 23 percent and 36 percent in secondary and tertiary industries, respectively. A drastic change occured in the Japanese labor force distribution during the following eight years. In 1963, the labor force engaged in primary industry was found to represent only 29 percent whereas 30 percent and 41 percent were engaged in secondary and tertiary industries, respectively.

I : JAPAN'S LABOR FORCE BY INDUSTRY

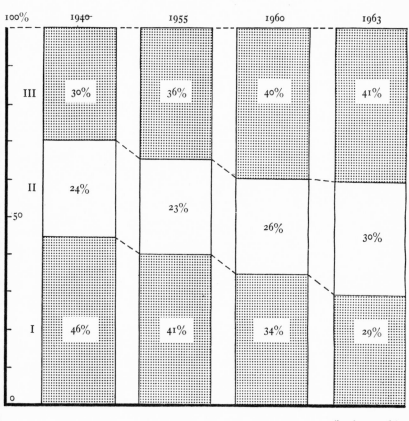

(in thousands)

	1940	1955	1960	1963
Total	32,231	41,190	44,610	46,130
I	14,789	17,040	15,000	13,370
II	7,823	9,380	11,870	13,860
III	9,619	14,770	17,740	18,900

Notes: I: Primary Industry
II: Secondary Industry
III: Tertiary Industry

Source: Japanese Government

2: INTERNATIONAL COMPARISON OF GROSS
NATIONAL PRODUCT (1962)

The Gross National Product in 1962 was $53,700 million, the fifth largest GNP in the free world.

Per capita GNP in 1962 was $564. On a simple comparison based on the official exchange rate, per capita GNP of Japan was about 20 percent of the American level, about 40 percent of that of West Germany, France and United Kingdom, and 70 percent that of Italy.

The average annual increase rate for the GNP between 1954 and 1962 was 9.4 percent. This was the highest in the free world.

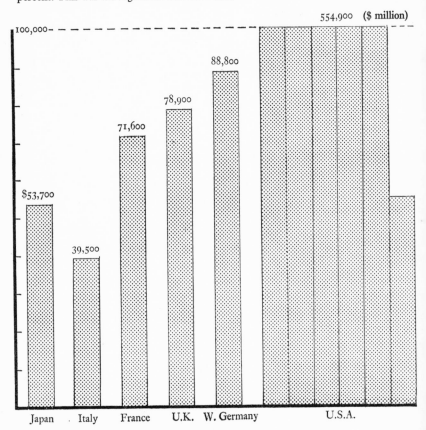

Sources: Statistics and Reports Division, Agency for International Development (U.S. Government), May 5, 1964, and Economic Planning Agency of the Japanese Government.

3: INTERNATIONAL COMPARISON OF GROSS NATIONAL
PRODUCT PER CAPITA (1962)

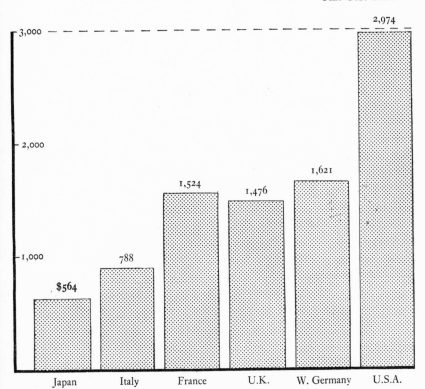

Unit U.S. doller

Sources: Statistics and Reports Division, Agency for International Development
(U.S. Government), May 5, 1964, and Economic Planning Agency of the
Japanese Government.

4: ECONOMIC GROWTH

By 1953, the Japanese economy had recovered to the prewar level.

This chart shows the growth in two of the main economic indicators over the past nine years, Gross National Product and per capita personal expenditure, expressed at constant prices.

The GNP in 1963 showed an increase at constant prices of 2.2 times over the 1955 figure. The increase rate in personal consumption expenditure per capita was more moderate, but its value in 1963 still showed an increase at constant prices of 1.7 times over 1955.

4: ECONOMIC GROWTH
Index at constant prices (1955=100)

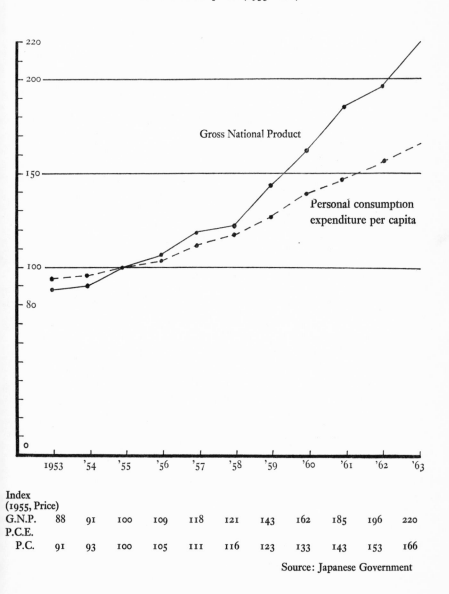

Gross National Product

Personal consumption
expenditure per capita

Index
(1955, Price)

	1953	'54	'55	'56	'57	'58	'59	'60	'61	'62	'63
G.N.P.	88	91	100	109	118	121	143	162	185	196	220
P.C.E.											
P.C.	91	93	100	105	111	116	123	133	143	153	166

Source: Japanese Government

5: INTERNATIONAL COMPARISON OF WAGES

6: REAL WAGE INDEX OF REGULAR EMPLOYEES

There are heated debates, internationally as well as domestically, as to whether or not Japanese labor is still cheap. However, Japan is no longer a low-wage country.

A simple comparison of the nominal hourly wages of manufacturing industry employees of Japan and other advanced countries at the official exchange rates shows that the wage level of Japan is a seventh of the American level and somewhat below that of France and Italy.

Moreover, the upward pace of Japanese wages has been very quick, as this chart shows. On an index basis, taking 1960 as 100, real wages of employees in establishments of 30 or more rose from 77 in 1954 to 112 in 1963.

5: INTERNATIONAL COMPARISON OF WAGES: JAPAN=100

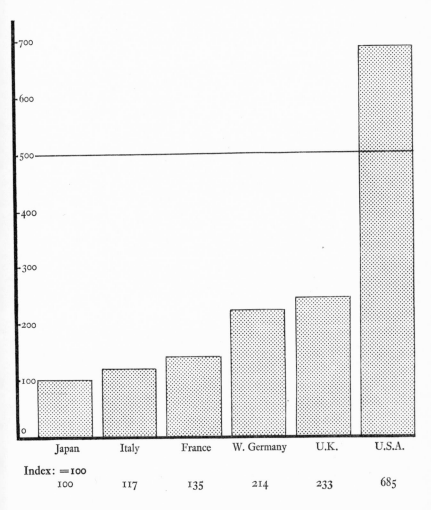

Index: =100

Japan	Italy	France	W. Germany	U.K.	U.S.A.
100	117	135	214	233	685

Note: Hourly wages of manufacturing industry workers in 1961, on the basis of the official exchange rate.

Source: ILO

6: REAL WAGE INDEX OF REGULAR EMPLOYEES
(Establishments with 30 employees or more)

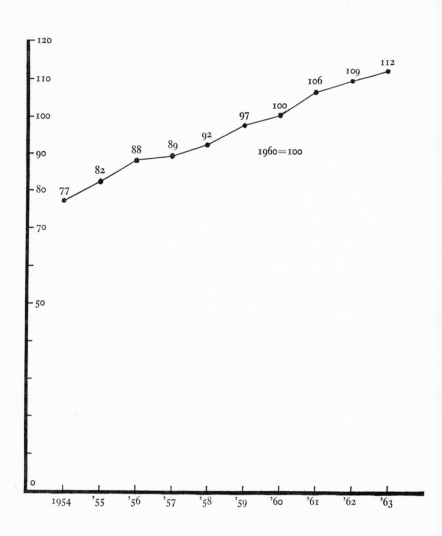

Source: Japanese Government

7: DIFFERENCE OF WAGES BY SIZE OF ESTABLISHMENT
IN MANUFACTURING INDUSTRY

In the smallest establishments too, shortage of labor has resulted in an increase of wage-rates, and the traditional wage-rate gap between large and small establishments has narrowed in recent years.

But this gap is still substantial, partly because a high percentage of the workers in the large establishments and to a lesser extent the workers in the medium-size establishments are given fringe benefits in various forms, such as free housing and recreation facilities, discount purchases of the daily necessities made available in their companies, etc., whereas most of the workers in the small establishments with less than 100 employees do not enjoy such fringe benefits. Out of the total number of paid employees in Japan, the workers in large establishments with 1,000 or more employees represent 18 percent, the workers in medium-size establishments with 100 to 999 employees 10 percent, and the remaining 72 percent are workers in small establishments with less than 100 employees. Labor should be regarded still as relatively cheap among this 72 percent, but it cannot be so regarded among the remaining 28 percent. The process by which this gap is being reduced at a fast rate in recent years can be seen in Chart 8.

7: DIFFERENCE OF WAGES BY SIZE OF ESTABLISHMENT
IN MANUFACTURING INDUSTRY, 1961 AND 1964

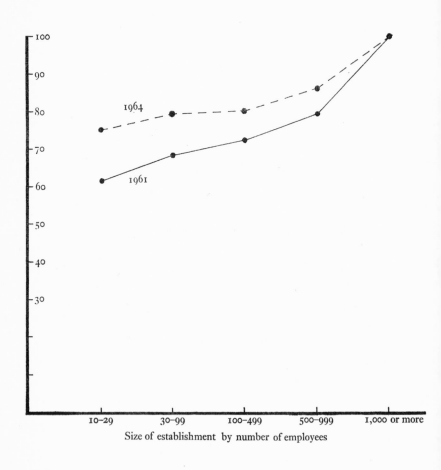

Size of establishment by number of employees

Index: 1,000 or more=100

1961	61	68	72	79	100
1964	75	79	80	86	100

Source: Japanese Government

8: CHANGING PATTERN OF INCOME DISTRIBUTION

A government sample survey to determine the people's employment status and the household income structure has been conducted every three years since 1959. The sample covers approximately 800,000 households throughout the country. According to the results of this survey, a considerable decrease in the number of low income households and a corresponding increase in the number of upper and middle income households was observed from 1959 to 1962. In 1959, there were 9.5 million households with an annual income below ¥200,000. The number of households belonging to this income class was reduced to 6.2 million in 1962. At the same time, the number of middle class households with annual income between ¥400,000 and ¥1,000,000 increased from 4.4 million to 8.2 million, and the number of upper class households with annual income over ¥1,000,000 increased from 0.4 million to 1.3 million.

The upper class and upper-middle class households are heavily concentrated in the two major markets, the Tokyo and Osaka areas. Of all the upper class households, 54 percent are in the Tokyo and Osaka areas combined, and 42 percent of all the upper-middle class households are in these areas. This means that the average standard of living is substantially higher in these areas than in the rest of the country.

8: CHANGING PATTERN OF INCOME DISTRIBUTION

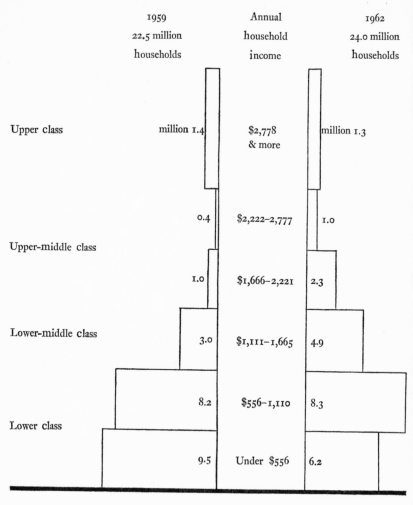

	1959	Annual	1962
	22.5 million households	household income	24.0 million households
Upper class	million 1.4	$2,778 & more	million 1.3
Upper-middle class	0.4	$2,222–2,777	1.0
	1.0	$1,666–2,221	2.3
Lower-middle class	3.0	$1,111–1,665	4.9
	8.2	$556–1,110	8.3
Lower class	9.5	Under $556	6.2

Note: $2,778 & more=¥1,000,000 or more
$2,222—2,777=¥800,000—999,999
$1,666—2,221=¥600,000—799,999
$1,111—1,665=¥400,000—599,999
$556—1,110=¥200,000—399,999
Under $556= under ¥200,000

Source: Japanese Government

9: INTERNATIONAL COMPARISON OF COMPOSITION OF
FAMILY EXPENDITURE

The growth of the national economy has resulted in a sizable improvement in people's living standards. To illustrate this, we show first recent changes in family expenditure composition, in particular the proportion accounted for by food. The proportion of the family expenditure for food (Engel's Coefficient) decreased from 48% in 1955 to 41% in 1961, and the proportion for housing and durable goods increased from 8% in 1955 to 12% in 1961. The proportion for "others," which includes education, medical care, recreation, and so on, also increased during the same period, from 28% to 30%.

Thus the whole pattern of the family expenditure in Japan has changed, as the standard of living has improved.

In making international comparisons, generally speaking, the lower the income the higher the proportion going into food. As shown in the chart, the Engel's Coefficient for the United States was 28% in 1962; in the United Kingdom and West Germany it was between 35% and 39%. In contrast to this, the Engel's Coefficient for Japan was 42%. Nevertheless, this figure is extremely low, when compared with Italy, whose incom elevel is similar to Japan. Thus it can be said that Japan is a country whose expenditure on food is low in comparison with income levels.

N

9: INTERNATIONAL COMPARISON OF COMPOSITION OF
FAMILY EXPENDITURE

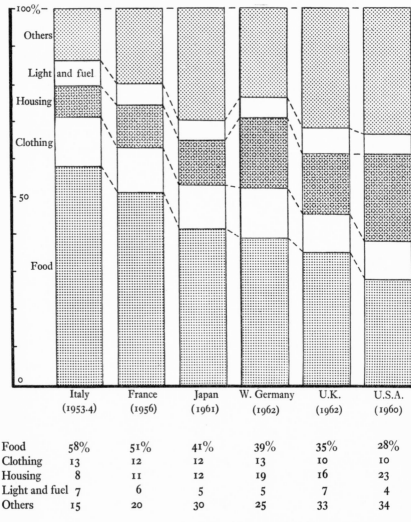

	Italy (1953.4)	France (1956)	Japan (1961)	W. Germany (1962)	U.K. (1962)	U.S.A. (1960)
Food	58%	51%	41%	39%	35%	28%
Clothing	13	12	12	13	10	10
Housing	8	11	12	19	16	23
Light and fuel	7	6	5	5	7	4
Others	15	20	30	25	33	34

Source: U.N. and Japanese Government

10: NET FOOD INTAKE PER CAPITA 1964
Calories per day

Japan's food consumption is inferior, both in quantity and quality.

The quantity of calories supplied per person, per day, is 2,290 calories, which is 20 to 30 percent lower than the 3,000 calories or so for countries in Europe and America. In content, moreover, the major portion is vegetable foodstuffs, whose value relative to animal foodstuffs is markedly small. The supply of animal foodstuffs in Japan is 260 calories per day, or only one-fifth of that of the United Kingdom or the United States.

Calories

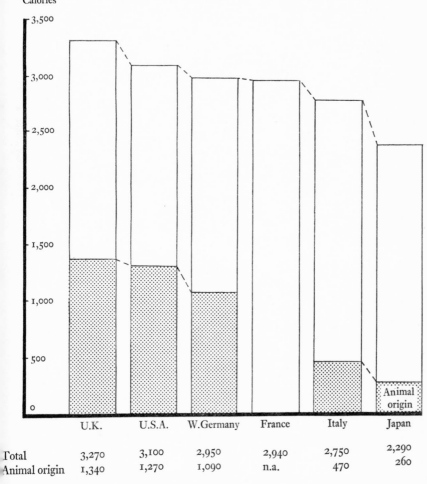

	U.K.	U.S.A.	W.Germany	France	Italy	Japan
Total	3,270	3,100	2,950	2,940	2,750	2,290
Animal origin	1,340	1,270	1,090	n.a.	470	260

Source: FAO

\

II : GROWTH IN CONSUMPTION OF CERTAIN WESTERNIZED
FOOD ITEMS

Although Japan's food consumption is inferior to that of western nations, a remarkable increase in consumption of westernized food items has been observed; compared with the consumption level in 1955, the consumption in 1962 was 4.3 times for green coffee, 3.8 times for pork, 3.6 times for beer, 3.5 times for chicken, 2.7 times for milk and dairy products.

II: GROWTH IN CONSUMPTION OF CERTAIN WESTERNIZE
FOOD ITEMS (1955=1)

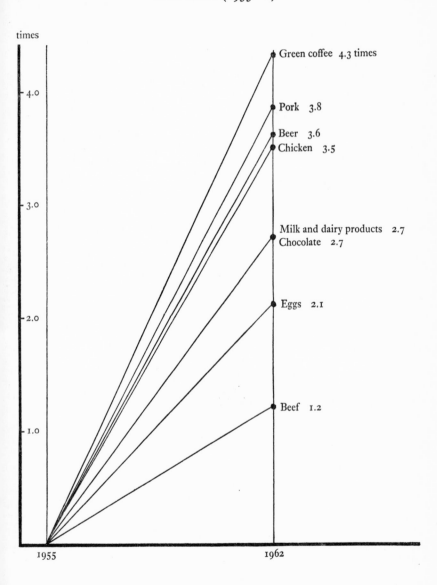

Source: Japanese Government

12: PER CAPITA ANNUAL CONSUMPTION OF TEXTILE
MATERIALS

The consumption of textiles per person, during 1963, was 7.9 kilograms. Compared with the 15.4 kilograms for the United States (1957) and the 12.9 kilograms for the United Kingdom (1957), the difference in quantity is not as large as the difference in per capita national income.

Out of 7.9 kilograms of textiles 2.5 kilograms or 32 percent was cotton, 2.0 kilograms or 25 percent was synthetic fibre fabrics, and 1.2 kilograms or 16 percent was wool.

12: PER CAPITA ANNUAL CONSUMPTION OF TEXTILE
MATERIALS

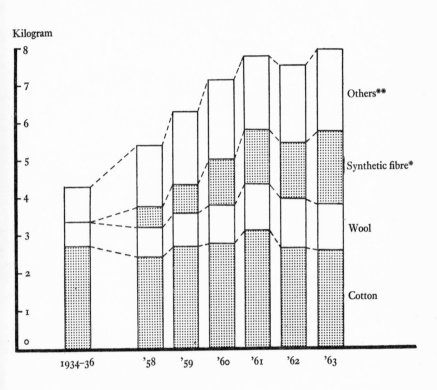

	Average in kilogram						
Total	4.22	5.37	6.26	7.09	7.68	7.43	7.87
Cotton	2.74	2.42	2.63	2.73	3.07	2.59	2.54
Wool	0.63	0.84	0.97	1.09	1.17	1.27	1.22
Synthetic fibre*	—	0.52	0.73	1.25	1.41	1.51	1.95
Others**	0.54	0.86	1.27	1.48	1.45	1.46	1.62

*—Including acetate fibre fabrics
**—Including silk, hemp, rayon fabrics and staple fabrics

Source: Japanese Government

13: CONSUMPTION OF FINISHED TEXTILE ITEMS IN
CITIES WITH 50,000 AND MORE POPULATION

Nowadays, most Japanese people wear western style clothes. Traditional *kimono* is worn by older people; young women wear the *kimono* only on special occasions such as weddings or New Year parties.

Thus, in 1963, expenditure on Western style clothes was three times that on *kimono*.

13: CONSUMPTION OF FINISHED TEXTILE ITEMS IN
CITIES WITH 50,000 AND MORE POPULATION
Annual purchases per household in US$

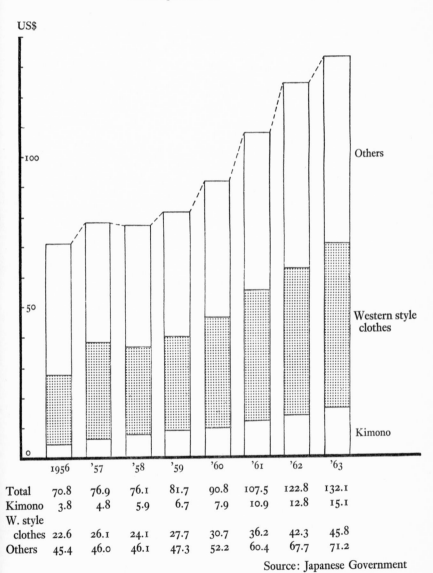

	1956	'57	'58	'59	'60	'61	'62	'63
Total	70.8	76.9	76.1	81.7	90.8	107.5	122.8	132.1
Kimono	3.8	4.8	5.9	6.7	7.9	10.9	12.8	15.1
W. style clothes	22.6	26.1	24.1	27.7	30.7	36.2	42.3	45.8
Others	45.4	46.0	46.1	47.3	52.2	60.4	67.7	71.2

Source: Japanese Government

14: PERCENTAGE OWNERSHIP OF HOME APPLIANCES

The pace of modernization of life manifests itself especially in the increasing ownership among Japanese households of such modern appliances as television sets, electric washing machines, electric refrigerators, vacuum cleaners and so on.

The penetration of television in the Japanese home during the past five years has been phenomenal. By February 1964, the household ownership of sets was found to be 88% or 20 million, which makes Japan the second largest television user in the world. As this chart shows, other appliances are also widely owned, in particular sewing machines and electric washing machines. The development of the Japanese electric appliances and camera industries has been strongly based on domestic consumer demand.

14: PERCENTAGE OWNERSHIP OF HOME APPLIANCES
FEBRUARY 1964

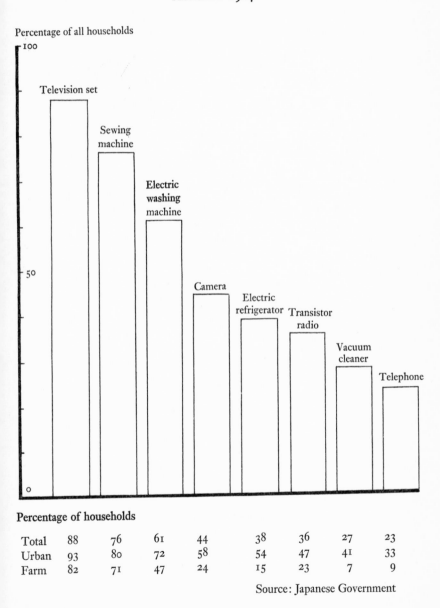

Percentage of all households

Percentage of households

Total	88	76	61	44	38	36	27	23
Urban	93	80	72	58	54	47	41	33
Farm	82	71	47	24	15	23	7	9

Source: Japanese Government

15: INTERNATIONAL COMPARISON OF NUMBER OF
PASSENGER CARS, 1962

Owership of passenger cars in Japan is relatively low when compared with Europe and the U.S. The number of passenger cars as of September 1964 was 1.5 million. The increase rate has been extremely fast; during the past 5 years it has been 30-40% per annum.

However, a "car-boom" on the scale of the electrical appliance boom has not yet occurred, and this development will surely represent the next stage of the Japanese consumer revolution.

15: INTERNATIONAL COMPARISON OF NUMBER OF
PASSENGER CARS, 1962

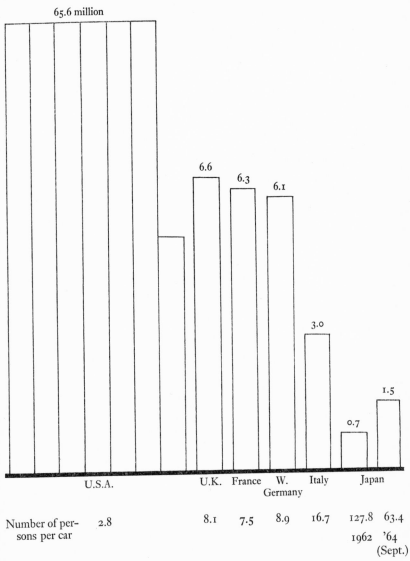

	U.S.A.		U.K.	France	W. Germany	Italy	Japan	
Number of persons per car	2.8		8.1	7.5	8.9	16.7	127.8	63.4
							1962	'64 (Sept.)

Sources: U.N. and Japanese Government

16: INTERNATIONAL COMPARISON OF HOUSING AREA
PER HOUSEHOLD IN URBAN AREA, 1962

The house size per household in urban area in Japan is 53 square meters, which is only about 60% of that of the United States or the United Kingdom. Moreover, the number of household members per household in Japan is considerably higher than in western countries, so living space per person becomes even smaller.

The greater part of the houses in Japan are wooden dwellings. Steel concrete dwellings are mainly built by the Public Housing Corporation, or the local governments.

16: INTERNATIONAL COMPARISON OF HOUSING AREA
PER HOUSEHOLD IN URBAN AREA, 1962

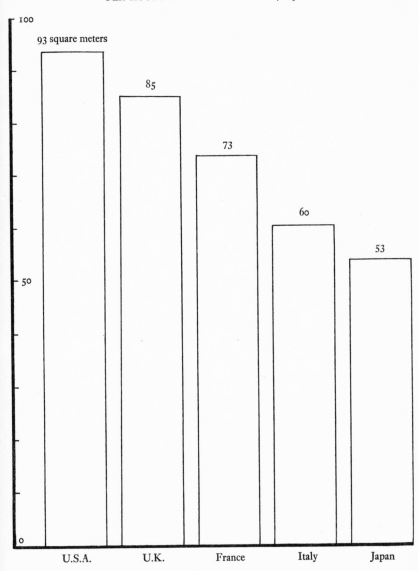

Source: Japanese Government

17: GROWTH RATE OVER THE PERIOD 1956 TO 1960 AND THE
SCOPE IN 1960, FOR EACH MAIN BUSINESS
TYPE OF RETAILERS

The rising standard of living is reflected also in the considerable growth of the retail trade. The Distribution Census showed that during four years since 1956, total gross retail sales increased by 44 percent and reached approximately ¥4,300 billion in 1960. The rate of growth varies by type of business. The highest growth was achieved in the "Furniture and Home Furnishing" field which more than doubled its sales during the period. Following this, the "Department Stores" field achieved an 89 percent increase in sales during the same period.

The distribution pattern in Japan is characterized by the existence of a very great number of small stores. In 1960, the Census showed that there were approximately 1.3 million retailers of all types throughout the country, and 3.4 million people were at work in these stores which altogether created the earlier mentioned gross annual sales of ¥4,300 billion. This means that only 2.7 workers were engaged in each store, producing gross sales of ¥3.3 million a year.

In general, the size of wholesalers is also small. In 1960 there were approximately 230,000 wholesalers in Japan, and 1.9 million people working in them. This means on the average only 8.4 people working in each wholesale store. These wholesalers are roughly classified into two groups. One consists of a relatively small number of large "first-stage wholesalers," whose areal coverage of trade is usually nation-wide. The other is comprised of a large number of small "second-stage" and third-stage wholesalers. The trade for each of these small wholesalers is limited to a certain town, village or part of a city. The structure of the distribution channels varies considerably from one type of business to another, and the whole pattern of distribution is extremely complicated. Such complication in the distribution results in relatively high distribution costs and low efficiency in the entire field of marketing. Improvement in this aspect has been much slower compared with improvement in the more tangible aspects of industrial techniques. However, certain indications of higher efficiency have begun to appear lately. As evidence, the Census shows that during the four years since 1956, the number of people engaged in retailing increased by 15 percent, and the number of stores increased only by 7 percent, whereas total gross sales increased by 44 percent.

This picture can be observed more clearly in grouping the retail stores, as well as wholesalers, according to the number of employees.

17: GROWTH RATE OVER THE PERIOD 1950 TO 1960 AND THE SCOPE
IN 1960, FOR EACH MAIN BUSINESS TYPE OF RETAILERS

(a) PERCENTAGE GROWTH RATE OVER THE PERIOD 1956 TO 1960

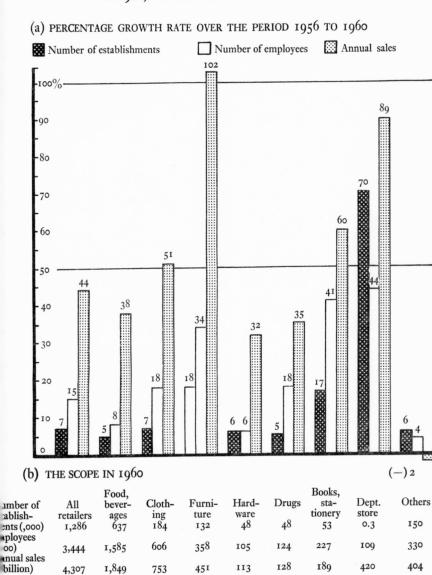

	All retailers	Food, beverages	Clothing	Furniture	Hardware	Drugs	Books, stationery	Dept. store	Others
umber of ablish- nts (,000)	1,286	637	184	132	48	48	53	0.3	150
ployees 00)	3,444	1,585	606	358	105	124	227	109	330
nual sales billion)	4,307	1,849	753	451	113	128	189	420	404

Source: Japanese Government

o

18: LARGE STORES IN TERMS OF NUMBER AND AVERAGE
MONTHLY SALES

During six years, from 1954 to 1960, the gross sales created by large retailers with 10 or more workers increased from 19 percent to 29 percent of the total for all retail stores, and the number of these large stores increased from 1 percent to 2 percent. Meanwhile, the share of small retailers with less than five workers decreased from 61 percent to 49 percent, and in terms of sales, from 94 percent to 91 percent, in terms of the number of stores. A similar trend is observed for wholesalers too.

18: LARGE STORES IN TERMS OF NUMBER AND AVERAGE
MONTHLY SALES

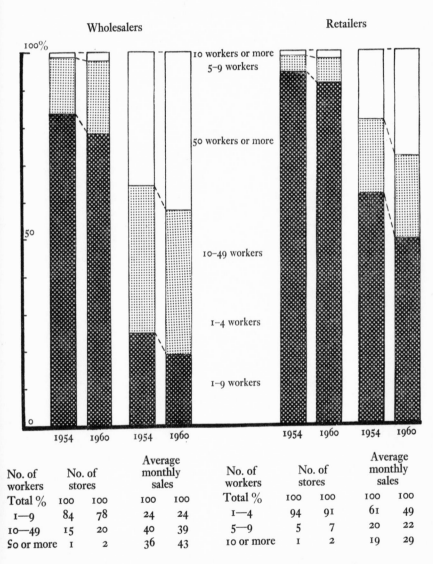

Wholesalers

Retailers

No. of workers	No. of stores		Average monthly sales		No. of workers	No. of stores		Average monthly sales	
Total %	100	100	100	100	Total %	100	100	100	100
1—9	84	78	24	24	1—4	94	91	61	49
10—49	15	20	40	39	5—9	5	7	20	22
50 or more	1	2	36	43	10 or more	1	2	19	29

Source: Japanese Government

19: NUMBER OF SELF-SERVICE STORES

Another indication of the trend towards greater efficiency in the distribution operation is the significant growth, in recent years, of a new type of grocery retailer operated on a self-service basis. Although not comparable in size and scope to supermarkets and discount stores in the United States, they are considerably larger in size and product range than the traditional retail stores in Japan, and they usually sell goods at discount prices; this is made possible by the reduction of operating costs and volume purchases from wholesalers or directly from manufacturers. One such store appeared in 1953, and the number rapidly increased in the following years, reaching 4,213 in 1964. It is predicted by certain specialists in the field that in five years time, 15 to 25 percent of the grocery sales in the country will be by this type of store alone.

A survey carried out under my supervision in 1962 showed that in Fukuoka, a city with 700,000 inhabitants in Kyushu, nearly 70 percent of the total sales of instant coffee in a particular month were actually created by 20 self-service stores and three department stores, and the remaining 30 percent were shared by 900 ordinary retail stores.

19: NUMBER OF SELF–SERVICE STORES

Number of stores

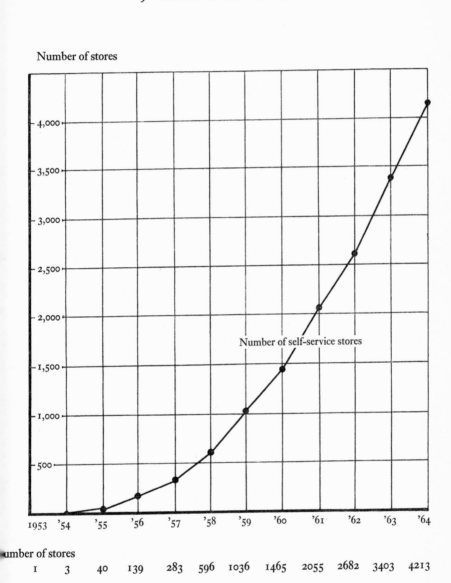

Source: Japan Self-Service Association

20: TEN WORLD LEADERS IN ADVERTISING VOLUME

Adversiting Age announced in a recent issue that Japan is fourth in advertising volume in the world, having spent $828 million for advertising in 1963. The advertising volume in 1964 showed an increase of 17 percent over that of 1963 and reached $970 million.

There are now almost all conceivable forms of advertising media in Japan, and their coverage is very extensive. Radio, television, newspapers and magazines blanket the country. Japanese consumers understand what they see and read, because the literacy rate is one of the highest in the world: 98 percent according to the Population Census in 1960.

Newspapers: there are 150 dailies, out of which 50 have evening editions of eight pages, as well as morning editions with 16 pages. These dailies have a combined circulation of 28 million copies. Out of the 150, four newspapers with national circulation represent approximately 50 percent of the total circulation, the top one, *Asahi*, with 4.1 million, *Yomiuri* 3.7 million, *Mainichi* 3.6 million and *Sankei* 1.9 million.

Magazines: there are approximately 800 consumer magazines which have a combined circulation of well over 40 million copies per issue, monthly or weekly. The most popular magazines claim circulations of nearly 1 million each.

Radio: there are approximately 19 million sets used in the home, not including 8 million transistor radio sets. There are 115 stations operated by the government and 130 commercial stations throughout the country. The Tokyo and Osaka areas are each covered by at least six channels, two governmental and four commercial.

Television: there are approximately 19 million sets used in the home. There are 78 stations operated by the government and 116 commercial stations. Tokyo and Osaka areas are each covered by six different channels, two governmental and four commercial.

20: TEN WORLD LEADERS IN ADVERTISING VOLUME, 1963

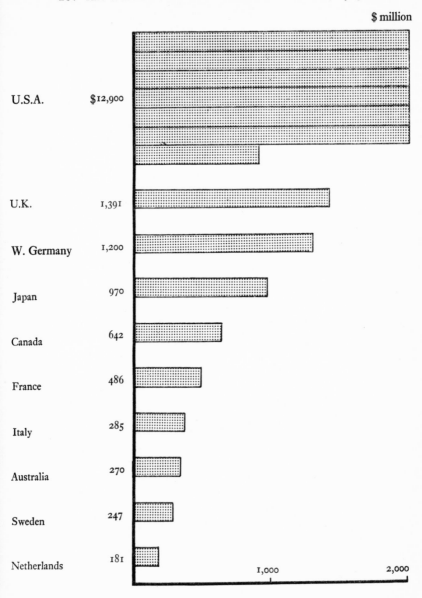

Source: *Advertising Age,* June 8, 1964

21 : ADVERTISING EXPENDITURES BY MEDIA

Advertising expenditures by media in 1962 were 38 percent in newspapers, 6 percent in magazines, 7 percent in radio, 28 percent in television, 4 percent in direct mail, and 17 percent in other media.

21: ADVERTISING EXPENDITURES BY MEDIA

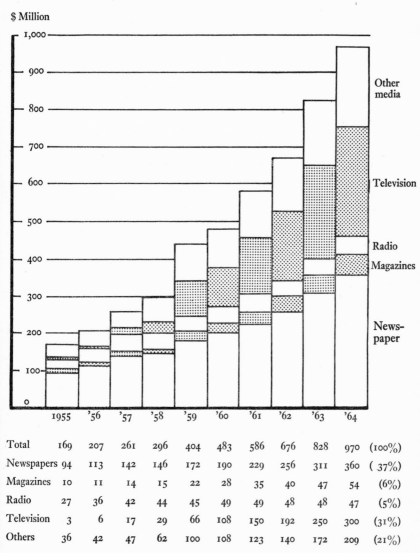

	1955	'56	'57	'58	'59	'60	'61	'62	'63	'64	
Total	169	207	261	296	404	483	586	676	828	970	(100%)
Newspapers	94	113	142	146	172	190	229	256	311	360	(37%)
Magazines	10	11	14	15	22	28	35	40	47	54	(6%)
Radio	27	36	42	44	45	49	49	48	48	47	(5%)
Television	3	6	17	29	66	108	150	192	250	300	(31%)
Others	36	42	47	62	100	108	123	140	172	209	(21%)

Source: Dentsu Advertising Agency

Index of Japanese Terms